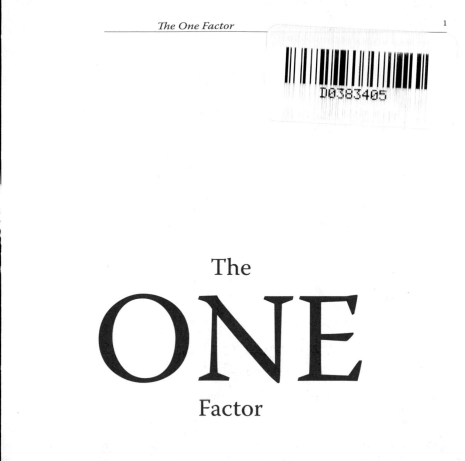

The

ONE

Factor

HOW ONE CHANGES EVERYTHING

The profits from the sale of this book have been designated to benefit the children in foster care in South Florida.

All the stories in this book are based on actual events, but many of the names have been changed.

Visit 4KIDS of South Florida's website at 4KIDSofSFL.org.

To the 4KIDS team, who battles every day on the front lines.

To Anitra and your incredible gift to turn

my random thoughts into intelligible English.

To my sons of thunder.

To Susi, the one I get to live the adventure with.

And to the ONE who makes it all possible.

Doug Sauder and the ministry of 4KIDS are daily reminders to me of the power of one. Whether you are a student, a corporate leader, or just someone anxious to know that you really can make a difference, I encourage you to discover the Source of the One Factor and how you can be the next "one."

—Bob Coy,
Senior Pastor of Calvary Chapel Fort Lauderdale

If you're convinced that one person can't change the world, get ready to be proven wrong. This book will have you looking at the people you meet, your appointments, your family and your life in a whole new light.

—H. Wayne Huizenga, Jr.,
Philanthropist and President of Huizenga Holdings, Inc.

I finished the first chapter of The One Factor, put the book down and wept over the story of Amber ... and I'm not a weeper. Reading on, however, gave me hope, and reminded me that one person with God is in the majority ... no matter the enormity of the battle. This is an inspirational book for everyone. Read it and reap.

—Dr. Bob Barnes,
President of Sheridan House Family Ministries

Caring for the orphans and widows is very close to the heart of Christ Jesus. Throughout our nation, the fatherless are crying out for love, hope, and someone to care for them. They are the forgotten and the invisible children. They are the modern day American orphan. The church must answer the call to rescue them in their time of peril and desperation. 4KIDS of South Florida and Place of Hope are reaching out to them with a cup of water in Jesus name. Together, we are making a lasting impact. My prayer is that Doug's book will serve as a reminder to the church that "the least of these among us" are a priority and that the many highlighted examples of compassion in action will serve to challenge us all.

—Dr. Tom Mullins,
Senior Pastor of Christ Fellowship and Founder of Place of Hope

The brother of Jesus, James, tells us not only what "pure and undefiled" religion looks like, but he also declares that "faith without works is dead." There is a genuine connection between the Good News and Good Deeds. "The One Factor" is a wonderful example of how God is using the Church to love orphans. It is a ONEDERFUL example of why good theology and people equity go hand in hand. If you want to see what it means to experience the reality of God in orphan ministry, read this book.

—Paul Pennington,
Executive Director of FamilyLife's Hope for Orphans,
a subsidiary of Campus Crusade for Christ, Chairman of
The Christian Alliance for Orphans Steering Committee

TABLE OF CONTENTS

FROM THE AUTHOR

Have you ever learned of a problem so great that you gave up on finding a solution before you put in any effort?

Global warming, AIDS in Africa, genocide, child abuse.

Sometimes the need is so overwhelming it paralyzes the mind. Resignation takes the place of hope, crippling your good intentions before they can get out of the starting gate.

Could my effort even make a difference?

Wouldn't it be like a raindrop falling into an ocean?

Unnoticed.

Unremarkable.

Insignificant.

If these thoughts have crossed your mind, then you're a lot like me. This book was written for both of us because we all need to be reminded that it only takes one to change everything. Just one.

I remember when I first heard it.

It was 1999, and I was a teacher in the public school system. I was sitting in church one Sunday when my pastor spoke about the crisis of "modern-day orphans." Children taken into foster care in our community were sleeping in offices because there were no foster homes for them. He said the Bible was clear about God's heart on this matter and that he wanted our church to do something about it. He told us that this was a solvable problem – if we all did our part.

As he spoke, my heart burned inside my chest. I knew I had to do something.

That one moment has taken me on a ten-year journey. Providing homes for modern-day orphans has become my driving passion. Through the years I have been inspired by others who dared to stare into the face of an overwhelming problem, fight through their feelings of helplessness, and then choose to act. Time after time I've seen "first steps" lead to unimaginable outcomes. This is the one factor—the power God unleashes when a solitary individual follows His call. I have seen the power of one tip the balance from staggering problem to attainable solution.

When I took that first step, I had no idea what I was getting into—the thousands of children who would receive shelter, the hundreds of young people who would experience a life-changing relationship with the God who made them, the dozens of children who would find a forever family ... and the one who would become my son.

This has been the most exhilarating thing I've ever done. One vision has changed my professional and personal life forever. This process has not been pain-free or easy, but then again, neither is life. This is a book born of the journey itself—about what can happen in a few short years to transform the biggest problem in your community, the biggest problem in your world.

I have no idea what one step there is for you, but I trust that within these pages, within these stories, the one thing God wants you to do will grow clearer.

And when He speaks to you, say yes.

Doug

*If you think you are too small to make a difference,
you have never spent the night with a mosquito.*
—Saying in Kenya

THE ONE FACTOR

How could one man chase a thousand?[1]
—Moses

THE HISTORY OF *ONE*

Does one vote make a difference?

Can one leader change the course of a nation?

Can one nation influence the history of the planet?

We've been taught that the answer is yes, but let's be honest—when it comes right down to it at election time, don't you secretly wonder, "Will my vote really matter?" As I drive to the polling booth, I have the strongest temptation to turn the car around and go home because my one little vote won't really swing the election, will it?

One has more significance than any of us realize. It has the power to make the small become big, when a seemingly insignificant straw suddenly breaks the camel's back. Consider the following *Ones*:

One Investment . . . 1492 . . . Columbus . . . Discovery

One Action . . . Rosa Parks . . . Bus Seat . . . Justice

One Idea . . . 2,000 Failures . . . Thomas Edison . . . Illumination

One affects thousands. *One* also has the power to make the big become small. It can reduce an insurmountable problem to a single face—the face that inspires the solution.

Slavery . . . Abraham Lincoln . . . *One* Nation

Polio Pandemic . . . Dr. Salk . . . *One* Vaccine

Aids in Africa . . . Bono . . . *One* Movement

World Poverty . . . Sponsorship . . . *One* Child

Thousands narrow to *one*.

A SOLVABLE PROBLEM

Every community has its problems. Think about the biggest problem in your world.

Can it be solved?

Most of us balk at the notion because many problems intimidate us by their sheer enormity. For the sake of this book, we will look at a huge problem that exists in every community—orphaned children.

Stop for a minute and review the scale of the problem:

143 million orphans worldwide

514,000 "temporary orphans" in foster care in America

115,000 "legal orphans" waiting to be adopted in America

This is a mind-blowing, heartbreaking reality that many of you might not have been aware of. Unfortunately, if you're like most of us, statistics like these rarely inspire action. As sobering as they are, they are too overwhelming, too impersonal, too distant. They may produce a twinge of guilt and maybe even provoke further research, but they rarely lead to action. Usually it is the one factor that gets us involved.

In the late 90s, it was difficult to pick up a South Florida newspaper and not cringe at the sight of another foster care disaster.

Children sleeping on office floors

Children sexually abused

Children missing

A state system bound with its own red tape was not equal to the task of caring for its most vulnerable members. There were simply not enough good foster homes for the hundreds of children who needed them. Homes were chronically overcrowded, and some families took children solely for financial gain. The eyes of the state and nation were riveted on this broken system.

THE SOLUTION

It starts with *one*. *One* is always the catalyst. It could be your neighbor who takes in Max, a foster child. Max plays with your kids. Sometimes he ends up at your house for dinner. He is now more than just an abstract foster care statistic. Max is real. You get to know his story, and you see his life being changed. One day something inside of you says, "I could do this!" There must be another Max out there.

What happens next can take you on a journey that will inspire others the way your neighbor unknowingly inspired you. The connection might seem linear. Your neighbor inspires you, and then you inspire someone else, who then inspires another. But the affect *one* has on others is usually more like an exponential web. Your neighbor is actually inspiring many others to get involved. The solution to the problem expands into a network with multiple connection points. An enormous problem is broken down to simple one-on-one relationships. The task is now possible. The mission, achievable.

This principle of the one factor is an empirical reality. Events throughout history have repeatedly proven it out, including what has happened in South Florida during the past ten years. We were a community plagued with an overwhelming foster care problem until *one* changed everything.

WHERE ARE WE GOING?

Throughout this book, we will explore the essential elements of the one factor to see how it can empower you to affect the lives of thousands, or even thousands of thousands.

One vision can take a shotgun approach and focus it into a single shot that can take down a charging beast.

One person can inspire another who inspires others, turning addition into exponential power.

One moment can turn the tide at the lowest point, when all seems lost, and inspire the courage to press on to victory.

One idea can create kinetic energy and momentum that turns a small rock into an avalanche.

One investment can lead to a series of returns that would make Wall Street green with envy—yields that will outlive you and your children's children.

One passion, like a virus, can contagiously inspire those who come into contact with it.

One Source makes it all happen. The power of *one* is not a product of chance.

If you've never really thought about the untapped potential of the power of *one*, I hope these stories will make you reconsider what you've considered insignificant. The one factor is all around you, waiting to be recognized and applied to your life. And once you become *one*, hang on because your life will never be the same.

ONE OF THOUSANDS

See that you do not look down on one of these little ones.
—Jesus

If we're using foster care as the case study of the one factor, then let's jump right in. This is Amber's story. It is one story out of a thousand. But we'll never understand the story of thousands until we understand one.

Amber's mom is a single parent. Her dad is long gone, and Amber is used to her mom's live-in boyfriends coming and going. Amber did her best to be a mom for her two younger sisters. It was hard when mom was passed out or simply didn't come home, but Amber knew the drill: make a few sandwiches, read a bedtime story, get her sisters ready for school the next day, and tell them everything was going to be all right.

Amber was very grown up for a nine-year-old, a fact not lost on one of her mom's boyfriends. At night he would sneak into her room and teach her secrets. Amber kept the shame all to herself. She thought her mom probably wouldn't believe her anyway, and she had to protect her younger sisters, so the abuse continued. The only person she told was a small stuffed bear, Teddy. At night she would cry into her pillow and whisper her secrets to Teddy.

Amber also talked to God.

She prayed that He would help her mom stop using drugs.

She begged God to keep mom's boyfriend away from her . . . but God never seemed to answer.

Then one day, in a drunken rage, her mom threw Amber against a wall and broke her arm.

The hospital noticed the fracture, along with some telling bruises, and immediately called child services. After several interviews, Amber and her sisters were removed from their mother's custody. [2] Mom's boyfriend was arrested. Finally things would get better for Amber.

Amber and her sisters were picked up by a caseworker named Ms. Jenna, who took all three girls back to her office. Ms. Jenna asked the girls to color some pictures while she made a few phone calls. Amber listened intently to the phone conversations:

"Do you have a home for three girls, age four, seven, and nine?" She watched as a frustrated Ms. Jenna put the receiver down and sighed. Amber recognized that look from her mom. Whatever it was, it wasn't good news.

It was painfully clear to Amber after the fourth call that nobody wanted her or her sisters. The day dragged on, and the uncertainty of where they would spend their first night away from home set in.

Finally, there was some good news. A home had been found. Ms. Jenna pulled Amber aside and told her there was a home for her sisters—but not for her. Amber's face flushed red-hot. She could not leave her sisters. They needed her.

Another caseworker came to take Amber's sisters to their foster home. They were inconsolable as they were placed in the car, crying for their big sister. Amber did her best to let them know that everything would be all right, even though she didn't really believe it herself.

Ms. Jenna continued to make calls until evening, but there was no home for Amber. Amber ended up staying in a hotel that night with another caseworker and in the morning was driven back to school. She looked for her sisters but didn't see them at lunch. That afternoon Ms. Jenna picked her up and told her that she would be staying in a shelter for a few days.

A few days turned into months.

The shelter had five rooms, but somehow twelve kids slept there. Amber was the youngest. The housemother didn't seem to like her job. She yelled at the kids for eating too much and always wanted them to go outside and stop making so much noise. Without Teddy and her sisters, Amber felt very alone. Sleeping in borrowed clothes, in a strange bed, with kids who were teaching her things she didn't want to know, Amber longed to be back with her sisters.

The court system gave Amber's mom a plan to earn the right to get her children back.[3] It included stipulations that she keep the boyfriend out of the house. Her mom showed up each month for supervised visits with Amber and her sisters, but not much else changed. Amber looked forward to the visits because they reminded her of what life used to be like. It was the only time she could see her sisters. She wished she could take those moments in time and freeze them. She couldn't wait for the day when they would be all back together for good.

Amber always looked forward to seeing Ms. Jenna. Her kind eyes made Amber feel at ease. But then one day Ms. Jenna told Amber she had some news. Her visits with her mom and sisters were stopping because the court had terminated her mom's rights. The family that had taken her sisters in was adopting them. She also told Amber that she wouldn't be seeing her as much anymore because she had found another job. The stress, low pay, and long hours had worn her out. She gave Amber her phone number and promised to keep in touch.

Amber was alone . . . again.

Her mom didn't want her enough to leave her boyfriend. Ms. Jenna left. Her sisters were taken from her. Teddy was left behind. Amber knew it was her fault—she was damaged goods. She was sure nobody would want someone like her. Maybe it would have been better if she were never born.

This is Amber's story, and it is very real. Now I want you to imagine something:

Amber is your daughter ...

... your sister

... your niece.

Until we see Amber that way, as a member of our own family, most of us won't respond. We may cry, but until we imagine our loved ones in her shoes, most of us will not act.

So are you mad?

Heartbroken?

Willing to open your home to Amber?

The system fails thousands of Ambers every year. The hope these "Ambers" have is extinguished, not because of the abuse they suffer, but because there is no one to intervene. Most people are oblivious to Amber's suffering; others are too busy, too indifferent, or too emotionally spent to care. But Amber only needs *one*.

When I saw what was happening to the Ambers of the world, I got angry. Things like this just shouldn't happen. Then I met a few people who were angrier than I was, but they had channeled their anger into energy. Their passion for justice and their focus on solutions created a synergy that sucked me in. It sucked a lot of us in. And then it unleashed a power greater than any one of us could have imagined.

I am not a rocket scientist, but this sounds a lot like nuclear fusion to me. It starts with a single atom. Energy is applied to that one atom, and soon atomic particles floating out there are attracted to that one atom. In a matter of time, this fusion becomes self-sustaining. It initiates a chain reaction with enough power to provide energy for thousands, or enough energy to destroy the entire planet. All this from one atom.

One initiates and leads to thousands of thousands. Have you ever gotten caught up in a chain reaction like this?

IT STARTED WITH ONE VOICE

*The only thing necessary for evil to triumph
is for good men to do nothing.*
—Edmund Burke

*I remember when I first met Irene. She was on a mission. Her
five-foot frame couldn't contain her passion to protect children.
It spilled over onto everyone around her. My wife and I were in
a foster parent training class she had organized. That's when I
first heard how it all began.*

Irene couldn't take it any more. She couldn't read another headline
and simply hope that the foster care system would change. But what
can one person do to change an enormous bureaucratic system? She
began to pray. A few days later she heard about churches in California
that had banded together to provide homes for children in foster care.
She knew this could happen in South Florida, too. She didn't know how
it would happen, but she knew she had to start somewhere. That day
she became one voice.

Irene knocked on every door she could find. Day after day she talked to
her friends, and even some strangers, about the situation. She continued
knocking until a door opened. One church listened to her vision and took

a chance.[4] With a handful of volunteers, an office, and a small budget, the movement began.

As the church's pastor, Bob, became more aware of the plight of foster care children in his own backyard, his burden for them grew. He approached his leadership and congregation with his desire to delay the planned opening of their Christian school. Instead, for one year the church would commit their resources to addressing this great community need. He shared his vision, and his congregation followed.

By the end of the first year, more than forty families from this one church had committed to taking children into their homes. By the end of the second year, another seventy-five families had joined the effort. Volunteers lined up, and donations began pouring in.

The growing momentum caught the attention of a local foundation who met with a group of community leaders to strategize long-term solutions. Together they crafted a plan and committed significant resources to make it happen.

The vision was in motion.

The synergy caught the attention of another advocate named Rick. A former foster parent, Rick wanted to see this vision impact every church in South Florida. Using the skills forged during his work mobilizing churches for hurricane relief, he implemented an ambitious plan.

Several houses were purchased, the staff doubled five times, and additional non-profits formed. Churches and community leaders throughout South Florida had joined the effort. The unlikely partnership of one church, one foundation, and a handful of individuals had brought the foster care crisis to a tipping point.

Ten years have gone by since Irene knocked on that first door.

It is hard for most to remember the hopelessness that existed just a decade ago. Although there are still problems in foster care, something has clearly changed. Where there was cynicism, now there is hope—and a genuine belief that the foster care crisis is a solvable problem. The Christian community is no longer intimidated by the idea of working with the state. Christians understand their biblical mandate to care for modern-day orphans and are mobilizing to meet this need.

With millions of dollars invested and hundreds of volunteers and churches now engaged, the results are clear . . . one has become thousands.

And that's how it happened. One woman acted. One pastor committed. One foundation invested. One man strategized. None of them could see where the next step would lead, but each responded nonetheless. And *one* changed everything.

This is that story.

ONE VISION

Progress should mean that we are always changing the world to fit the vision, instead we are always changing the vision.
—G. K. Chesterton

Maybe you've heard this illustration: How do you tackle a huge problem? The same way you eat an elephant . . . one bite at a time.

But as you begin to take bites, it's easy to lose the big picture in the process. A clear vision is essential to keep you from losing sight of the goal.

I can't tell you how many visions I've seen fall by the wayside because the people were trying to address every issue of a particular problem, accomplishing very little in the process. This shotgun approach is like spraying an elephant with a hundred BB's. It may sting, but he'll keep charging. On the other hand, a single well-placed shot with the right bullet can stop an elephant in his tracks.

When we first looked at the problem of foster care in our community, we knew we needed a clear vision. But where should we start? Our instinctive response was to protect. We had to find a place where we could meet the needs of children after they were taken from their families. We knew we must end the waiting in administrative offices or hotels.

So we created SafePlace, a twenty-four-hour "super shelter" that serves every child taken into foster care. But protection was only part of the solution. We couldn't lose our focus.

Often there weren't enough foster homes for these kids to go to from SafePlace. So we spread the word about the need for more foster parents and watched the training classes begin to fill up. We also created a series of family-style homes in regular neighborhoods where kids could live with houseparents for one to three months. But that was still not enough.

These were temporary solutions. We didn't want to keep kids in foster care. Our mission was to move them toward a permanent solution . . . a family. We did this through identifying the three possible outcomes for kids in foster care: re-unification with their family, adoption into a new family, or independent living for kids who turned eighteen and were still in foster care.

Our vision was to create a system without gaps.

This is where the one factor was a great ally. It helped us avoid the shotgun approach of trying to meet every need of every child and allowed us to focus our energy on giving children a family. Instinctively we knew that if children were placed in loving families, they would have everything they needed. Our goal was that at every stop in a child's foster care journey, a family would be ready to give the hope that he or she had been robbed of.

Remember the elephant? We knew we needed a clear paradigm for tackling the foster care crisis—create families, provide hope. By narrowing our focus, we were able to say no to many good things because they were not what we did best. You can see it in our vision statement:

"A home for every child in crisis."

THE TRAUMA UNIT

For he will conceal me there when troubles come;
he will hide me in his sanctuary.
He will place me out of reach on a high rock.[5]
—David, King of Israel

Imagine how you would feel if you were removed from the only home you had ever known. A police car pulls up late at night and there is a loud knock at the door. The next thing you know you are being shuttled off to an unknown place, all your possessions stuffed into a garbage bag. This is how a thousand children every year arrive at SafePlace, our round-the-clock trauma unit. They each arrive with a different story, but their pain is much the same. There is nothing "heart warming" about a trauma unit, but everyone is grateful it's there when they need one.

The following is a log of a typical day on the front lines:

6:00AM Staff and volunteers arrive for prayer. They get updates from the overnight staff and pass a high five to encourage their comrades after a difficult night.

6:15AM A staff member wakes the children in need of medical appointments. Another staff member checks the rest of the sleeping children.

6:30AM A few staff members organize showers for those who arrived in the middle of the night. A volunteer prepares breakfast.

7:00AM As the children wait for breakfast, they sit in the playroom. Some watch a movie, others listen as a volunteer reads a book, and others play with toys. One child sits completely alone in a corner, quiet and withdrawn, ignoring any attempts by the staff to interact.

8:00AM Sheriff's officers arrive with three more children in need of care. The children have lice, and a staff member acts quickly to isolate and treat them. Then the meticulous sanitization process begins to prevent contamination of any other children or staff.

8:30AM The children in need of medical care are picked up by their caseworkers for medical screenings.

8:45AM An eleven-year-old girl, overcome by her circumstances, retreats to a closet and bangs her head against the wall. A staff member tries to reassure the girl that she is safe but is unable to calm her down. A mobile crisis unit is called to have the child removed for a mental health evaluation.

10:00AM A crack-addicted baby is rocked continuously by a volunteer, desperately trying to comfort the child who seems unaffected by her efforts. A tear streaks down the volunteer's face as she sings "Jesus Loves Me" and wonders if the baby's mother even realizes how much pain she has caused her child.

12:00PM As lunch is served, a pregnant teenager gets into a heated argument with another teen. Plates fly, and the teens have to be separated.

1:00PM After phone calls throughout the morning, the attempts to place these children into foster homes finally yield some results. Three children find a home with an aunt. Another child is placed in an open foster home. A sibling group of three is unable to be placed together and must be separated. The six-year-old youngest brother is inconsolable as he watches his older brother and sister leave with the caseworker. For the eight remaining children, frustration and anxiety increases.

3:00PM A four-year-old girl arrives from the hospital with a broken arm. The hollow look in her eyes clearly reveals that she is still in shock. A staff member utters a silent prayer for this young girl as she is guided to the playroom.

4:00PM Another staff member continues to make phone calls to shelters and foster homes, looking for places that will take the children, but the answers continue to be no.

4:30PM A seventeen-year-old girl arrives. She had been locked in an apartment for days, with no outside communication. Her mother sold her to a drug dealer to purchase more drugs. The girl is unresponsive to the staff.

5:00PM An eight-year-old sexually abused girl arrives. Her mannerisms are very seductive and aggressive toward the male staff. A volunteer pulls her aside to talk with her about her behavior. She is the eleventh child to arrive that day.

6:00PM Volunteers arrive and begin to prepare dinner, while fresh staff takes over for their exhausted counterparts.

6:30PM Dinner is served as volunteers try to help kids with homework, make phone calls, and clean up after a long day. The six-year-old boy who was separated from his brother and sister asks a staff member to pray for them.

7:00PM Beds at a shelter have opened up for three more children. The staff hustles to get their things together so they can meet the van waiting to transport them to their next stop on their foster care journey.

8:00PM The children take showers, and a few extra cots are set up. SafePlace is still full, even after seven children have been placed in homes; eleven children will stay overnight.

9:00PM The young children are put to bed, with stories and hugs. As the staff tries to finish the required paperwork, a teenage girl approaches a staff member and asks sarcastically, "Why would God let this happen to my family?" The twenty-minute conversation that follows produces a change in the young girl's attitude as she genuinely fights to understand that God does see, He does care, and it won't always seem this hopeless. The briefest smile runs across her face as she realizes that although there are few visible reasons for it, somehow, strangely, hope still exists.

10:00PM All is quiet as the overnight staff arrives, exchanges notes, and relieves their tired co-workers.

It begins again . . .

6:00AM With the exception of a four-year-old who woke up from a nightmare in an unfamiliar place, it has been a quiet night. The overnight staff updates the incoming staff and volunteers, and it starts all over again . . . another day on the front lines.

When staff and volunteers first start serving at SafePlace, most don't sleep very well for the first few weeks. How do you stop your mind from thinking about each of the faces you saw the day before? Childhoods lost, children with so much promise torn apart. Yet, for all the children who have had their hearts and bodies bruised and battered, SafePlace is a refuge they will never forget. Many of them still speak of that twenty-four-hour stay years later. For most of them it was a starting-over point— a point they were protected through ordinary people willing to extend themselves, one child at a time.

THE HOUSE ON THE CORNER

By wisdom a house is built, and through understanding it is established; through knowledge its rooms are filled with rare and beautiful treasures.[6]
—Solomon

The child is now safe. He has been protected. His needs have been assessed. Now he needs provision.

The paradigm of foster care in our community was to place this child in a large shelter that held twenty or thirty children. Our vision is to place him in a home—the best place to give him the dignity he deserves and the hope he needs.

The house that became KidsPlace was a neighborhood eyesore until it was purchased and renovated through a partnership between a community church and a local family foundation. In the first five years of operation, two hundred children have called KidsPlace home. Its rooms have witnessed more than their share of miracles.

The house on the corner was abandoned. The paint was chipped and faded, the yard overrun with rocks and weeds, and the walls streaked with mildew from a leaky roof. Neighbors passed by without a second glance.

Few were left who remembered when the house had been full of life and activity.

So much potential . . . neglected, wasted, lost.

TJ was abandoned, his life wounded and broken. His once infectious smile was faded by rejection and abuse. Once vibrant eyes were dimmed by sights no child should see. His hollow gaze reflected a lost innocence. Few remembered when his heart bubbled up with joy, and his laughter filled the air.

So much potential . . . neglected, wasted, lost.

Then one day something in that neighborhood changed. The house had a new owner. The yard was full of friends laying sod, replacing dry-wall, loading furniture, and cleaning the pool. Neighbors were anxious to meet the new family; the only clue to their identity was a cross etched into each of the gateposts. The house was almost finished, its rooms now restored and ready to welcome kids.

TJ was one of the first to arrive, dragging a black garbage bag filled with his possessions. He'd once shared a bed with swarming roaches, but the sheets on his new bed felt crisp and clean. The rocket-ship mural on his bedroom wall fueled his imagination. TJ ate home-cooked meals on the new kitchen table. He swam in the pool and played foot-ball in the backyard. He learned that getting an A can make homework worth the effort. TJ's life has been restored. His heart is ready to wel-come love.

If TJ's room could talk, it would tell of the nights he cried himself to sleep and the days he raged and screamed as he learned to accept love and discipline as part of a family. It would tell of the afternoon with his counselor when the secrets he had promised never to tell came pouring out. It seemed like the tears would never stop. TJ's room would speak of the purpose he had rediscovered there, of hope reborn. TJ's infec-tious smile is all the proof you need that provision is more than just food, clothes, and shelter.

A boy and a house. Both needed *one* to bring them back to life. Both needed someone who could see past the surface, to the great potential within. Now when the neighbors pass by, they take a second look. The boy and the house both look remarkably different. There is a word for this process of transformation—redemption.

TJ's room used to have a sign on the door that read, "Keep Out!" Now there's a new sign. It reads, "God Lives Here!"

WHEN HOPE WON'T DIE

Of all the forces that make for a better world, none is so indispensable, none so powerful, as hope. Without hope men are only half alive. With hope they dream and think and work.
—Charles Sawyer

I talk a lot about the value of hope and its power to give a person courage. Its ability to allow someone to persevere under horrific conditions and in the face of overwhelming odds. But I have to admit that sometimes I lose hope for certain people, especially the parents of kids in foster care. I see the havoc their selfish choices have wreaked on their children. We've all heard stories about children returning from foster care to their biological parents, only to be re-abused.

It seems so senseless. But the truth is, most kids in foster care will return to their families.

One of our primary goals is to make sure they return to a family that is restored and supported. Re-parenting adults who have had their lives filled with dysfunction for so long doesn't always yield the results we hope for. And that can make you cynical. It can make you want to give up on people. To be honest, it can make you almost hope they don't succeed. But then there are stories like Kelly and John's ... a story that reminds me that every one of us needs a second chance.

Kelly was in a Phoenix jail awaiting sentencing on a felony conviction when he held his two-week-old son, John, for the first time. Although it was only for thirty minutes, Kelly memorized every detail of his son's tiny features. He knew he was facing up to fourteen years in prison, with no expectation of parole for at least seven years.

Kelly's desire to be a good father drove him to earn his associate's degree and attend parenting and anger-management classes. After four years behind bars, he was hopeful at his first parole hearing. He had been a model inmate. Surely the parole board would see he had changed. His son needed him.

But Kelly's parole was denied.

Year after year the same scenario played out. Because the parole hearing was in December, Christmas always meant dashed hopes.

A few of his friends invited him to a Bible study where he heard about the Angel Tree program. Every year at Christmas, prisoners could sign up their children to receive gifts purchased and delivered by volunteers in the name of the imprisoned parent. The program gave Kelly a glimmer of hope. He needed his son to know he loved him and was trying to reach out to him.

So every year Kelly signed John up for a gift. Some years the volunteers reported that they were unable to locate John. Some years they wrote and told Kelly how grateful his family was for the gifts.

After fourteen years of tormented Decembers, Kelly was released. He had served every single day of his sentence. His contact with John over the years had been sporadic—a few letters, some monosyllabic phone conversations, and an occasional Father's Day card.

Within days of his release, Kelly got a frantic call from his ex-wife saying he needed to come to Florida immediately if he ever wanted to see his son again. Facing her own prison sentencing, she was concerned John would be placed into foster care. Kelly contacted a friend from prison now living in South Florida. The friend immediately offered to pick Kelly up at the airport, give him a place to stay, and help him find work in the area. He also invited Kelly to his church, where he found acceptance and support.

Because of his mother's difficulties, John was living with his grandmother and had already been assigned a foster care caseworker. Kelly's intention all along was to seek custody of his son, and he immediately began working on his re-unification plan—the court-determined steps that would allow him to be considered for custody.

Kelly met with John for the first time since that day when he had held him as a baby fourteen years earlier. It was an awkward attempt to get to know this virtual stranger, but Kelly was determined to start the process of making up for lost time. Two weeks after Kelly arrived in Florida, he received a call from his ex-wife notifying him that her mother, who had been caring for John, had died suddenly. Because there was no room for John at SafePlace, he was taken by police car to jail, where he spent the night.

John finally made his way to an emergency shelter. The houseparents there agreed to a supervised visit with Kelly at a local church. Kelly was so glad to see his son again and felt at ease with John's houseparents. They encouraged Kelly in his efforts to obtain custody and worked with him over the next several months until he was awarded custody of his son.

And now, for the rest of the story.

Remember the Angel Tree volunteers who delivered Kelly's gifts to his son? Remember the friend from prison who invited Kelly to stay with him in South Florida? Remember the houseparents who helped ease the transition for a dad who needed help with his teenage son?

They were all connected. They all attended the same church. Coincidence?

I think it's something more than that.

In Kelly and John, we see something bigger than coincidence working outside of our immediate view, weaving people, places, and circumstances into a tapestry that, in the end, is beautiful beyond description. In a story that stretches from Arizona to Florida, from a gift for Christmas to a place called home, from a father holding a baby boy for the first time to an awkward conversation with a teenage son—this is more than a coincidence.

It is evidence of hope's source.

Kelly is my reminder that we need to have hope for more than just foster kids. Their parents have their own stories, and if we are serious about helping kids, then we have to be willing to be a part of their parents' stories too. Kelly and John are making the most of their second chance, surrounded by an engaged support system. At first glance, their story looked like another lost cause—another absent father abandoning his son.

But if I look past my faulty assumptions and beyond my limited perspective, I will find a reason to hope. Kelly and John's story reminds me of this truth. When I see a broken family next week, I'll remember that hope is alive and well and that God is at work, making the mess into something beautiful.

Making redemption happen.

"YOU'RE GONNA LOVE IT HERE!"

I am going there to prepare a place for you . . .
I will come back and take you to be with me . . . [7]
—Jesus

Among abandoned and neglected children, the most vulnerable are those who are medically needy. Having a chronically ill child can place an enormous strain on the whole family. Some medically fragile children enter foster care after their parents have struggled for years to care for them, while others go straight from the hospital to a shelter—their parents overwhelmed by the prospect of 24-hour care.

As a child, I watched my parents care for my younger brother, Daniel, who was born with a genetic disorder. It affected every body system, leaving him unable to talk or even roll over. Fragile and prone to sickness, the slightest cough could hospitalize him for weeks. Countless hospital visits marked his short six-year life, which he lived as a virtual infant.

A few years into our marriage, my wife and I had our first son, Jordan. He was born with the same disorder. Shock doesn't begin to describe it. Life on hold. Months in the hospital. Sleep deprivation. Specialists. Opinions. Pressure. Planning a funeral for our nine-month-old son.

We went through all this because Jordan was our son, and we loved him. But I can't imagine volunteering for this duty. If Jordan wasn't my son, I wouldn't have signed up for that. I'm not that sacrificial. There isn't a long line forming to adopt children like Daniel and Jordan, but I have a friend and co-worker who can't let a child languish alone.

Mat and his wife, Spring, are the kind of people that do crazy things like getting in line.

Here is their story in their own words:

It's been three years since our first foster son, Jay, came to live with us. It seems like a lifetime ago that we were preparing the crib, the car seat, the clothes. Because Jay was HIV positive and medically fragile, those preparations were multiplied. We visited the medical shelter where he had lived the first eighteen months of his life and watched the nurses' every move. We learned to give the g-tube feedings, monitor his breathing, take his blood pressure, give his nebulizer treatments, and offer the percussive blows to his back and chest that would allow him to remain clear of pneumonia. After weeks of training we were finally ready to bring him home. We welcomed him with both elation and apprehension.

As we drove to the downtown shelter to pick up Jay, we pondered the gravity of the moment. Instinctively, we knew that this decision and this young boy would change our lives forever. After filling out the final paperwork, we slipped Jay into the back seat. You could see apprehension on his face. He was leaving the only home he had ever known. The drive to our home was filled with front-seat conversation, trying to get Jay to laugh or talk. Despite our best efforts, the backseat was quiet the entire ride home.

Over the next few weeks, we experienced the joy of discovery, the likes of which we have never witnessed before or since. Jay quizzically sniffed the carpet. Jay was swallowed by the recliner. At the medical shelter, his world was a room with two cribs, a few toys, and walls lined with medical equipment. When we brought Jay outside, he walked barefoot on grass for the first time. Sights, smells, tastes, and sounds filled him with wonder. We could tell by his inquisitive look and smile that Jay loved his new world. As first-time parents, Jay opened up a whole new world for us also. That world got bigger a year later when we adopted him.

A few years later, when Jay was five and thriving, we began to consider adding to our family again. God directed us to another shelter, where we met our second foster son, Charlie. Because of his special medical and behavioral needs, we made the same visits we had done with Jay. After several weeks the big day arrived. We piled into the car for the downtown trip to bring Charlie home. This time there were three of us. I asked Jay if he was excited about getting a new brother. True to his nature, Jay answered without words, just a quick nod and a slight grin.

As we pulled up to the shelter, we could see Jay's mind racing as he waited quietly in the back seat. He watched in silence as we loaded all of Charlie's belongings into the trunk and buckled him in next to Jay. We attempted to engage Charlie in conversation. Jay, always pensive, quickly picked up on Charlie's anxiety. It was obvious that Jay wanted to say something to ease Charlie's tension, but his painfully shy nature prevented the words from coming.

In the rearview mirror, we could almost see his mind replaying the uncertainty of the ride he had taken a few years earlier. He struggled to offer a word of comfort, but nothing came out. After we pulled out of the shelter, courage trumped fear—and he uttered the words we will never forget, the words that let Charlie know everything was going to be all right:

"You're gonna love it here!"

(Six months later we adopted Charlie.)

GIFT-GIVERS

Heroism is not only in the man, but in the occasion.
—Calvin Coolidge

How do you react when you hear of a woman who walks into an adoption agency and gives her child away? At first glance it seems almost heartless, but when you take the time to listen to her story, another word comes to mind—courageous.

To the mom who makes this agonizing decision, it is not a child given away, but a gift given—a gift to a family desperate to love a child and a gift to her child that she is unable to give. In a way, these mothers have stronger maternal instincts than moms who choose to tough it out, keeping their children for purely selfish reasons. For many, the decision to place a child for adoption ultimately saves a child from entering foster care and the scars that often accompany that journey.

I never would have tried to understand the struggle of a birth mother if I hadn't sat across from a brave teenage girl named Melinda nine years ago. On my twenty-ninth birthday, this young girl handed me and my wife a beautiful baby boy and said to us through sobs, "Take good care of him." When I got home I couldn't stop looking at Jackson's face, but I didn't expect to be thinking about Melinda. She had just given me the best birthday gift I would ever receive.

Here are two more stories of gift-givers like Melinda.

FRIENDS WITH BENEFITS

My name is Collette, I'm twenty-one years old, and I'm about halfway through my senior year in college. I want to teach elementary school one day. I've always loved kids, and I think I'll really be a natural. All my young nieces and nephews have always looked up to me, and I know that teaching is what I'm meant to do.

I haven't had what you would call a steady relationship since high school. But Eddie and I enjoy each other's company, and we agreed that we would just be friends, as they say, with benefits. It seemed harmless enough; no strings attached. After all, we weren't hurting anyone.

Then I got pregnant. Eddie was in a panic, tearing through the phone book looking for a way to "get rid of the problem," as he put it. I listened on the extension while he called a list of abortion clinics, my emotions racing from relief to horror as they described their various methods of "helping us." I thought, How ironic. Here I am spending every waking moment struggling for a career where I can make a difference in the life of a child, and at the same time I'm actually considering taking the life of my own.

After we hung up from the last call, Eddie and I sat in total silence for what seemed like forever. Then we had what was probably the most honest conversation of our entire relationship. Why should this tiny baby inside of me have to pay with her life for our irresponsible behavior? What began as a very helpless feeling quickly evolved into a realization that we were in a very powerful position.

After a few days we contacted an adoption agency. They gave us a picture album of couples who were waiting to be good parents, most of whom had experienced years of infertility and heartbreak. After reading a profile on each couple, we chose a family we thought would be best for our daughter. This process helped us make sense of my pregnancy. We knew she was not an accident; she had a greater purpose.

Vivian was born one week before my scheduled due date, and the couple we chose was able to come to the hospital shortly after she was born. I will always treasure in my heart what my child's adoptive mommy said to me that day, as she held my precious little angel in her arms: "Now I know why we waited so long to be parents; it was for this special child. Thank you."

NEVER TOO LATE

My name is Austin, I am twenty-seven years old, and I have a ten year-old son. His mother, Nancy, and I are trapped in a life of addiction, so he has been living with friends of my family on and off for years now. This is not what we wanted for Brad, but placing him with a family stopped him from being taken into foster care.

Now he is at the age where we can see that it is becoming very confusing for him to go back and forth. We realize we are being irresponsible parents, having him with us when we have "good" months, only to have to send him away when things get bad again. He deserves to know that he has a stable home and people who will always be there for him.

Nancy and I have recently made the incredibly hard decision to voluntarily surrender our rights and allow Brad to be adopted by a wonderful family. This was not an easy or careless decision; we love our son. We have spent many nights agonizing over this. Our son did not choose to be born to parents who were not prepared to give him the stability and guidance he deserves. We've made many bad decisions in our lives. It is time to stop being selfish.

Brad will never have to worry about a roof over his head or having enough food in the refrigerator. He won't miss a ride to school because his parents are too hung over. We are giving our son the gift of adoption so he can grow up in the home he has always deserved and become all he was meant to be.

WAITING

Every long lost dream led me to where you are . . .
God blessed the broken road that led me straight to you.
—Lyrics from "Bless the Broken Road"

I remember when I first met Mez. Our church was sponsoring an adoption-matching party, where children who were waiting for an adoptive home interacted with prospective adoptive couples. For the younger kids, it was a great afternoon of eating and playing games. Most of them were oblivious to what was taking place, but a teenager named Mez knew exactly what was happening—and what was at stake.

I noticed him standing near the food table, and I casually approached him and asked if he was having a good time. He nodded. After a brief conversation he cut to the chase: "Really, Doug, who is gonna want to adopt a fifteen-year-old?"

Mez had been to these parties before and had never been picked to be part of a family. He abruptly changed the subject, so I suggested we head over to the basketball court. After a good game we talked briefly and then parted ways. But I couldn't get his words out of my mind.

Three years later I met Mez again. He had never gotten the family he had hoped for. He was eighteen and needed a place to live because he had aged out of foster care. With nowhere to turn, Mez came looking for us. I made sure we had a place for him this time.

Our vision had caught up with Mez.

We had just launched an independent-living program to provide housing for former foster children. He moved into one of our homes for young men, and there he found his family. It wasn't the family either of us had envisioned on that hot summer day, but God had a plan that surprised us both.

This is Mez's story in his own words:

I sit, and I wait. Glancing to the left, I wait and think. I search the horizon for that tiny row of yellow lights visible above the endless stream of glowing white lights.

The bus should be here soon. I hope it's on time. It's chilly tonight.

I can feel the cold metal bench through my jeans as a light rain spits down from a dreary sky. I seem to spend my life waiting for others. Random thoughts fill my head.

Will it be busy at work tonight? PlayStation 3 is coming out. I wonder what my ex-girlfriend is doing. Lord, how did I ever get here?

I know these streets well, too well. These streets raised me. My arms and chest carry the physical scars of my street upbringing. My heart bears the scars of my desperate hunger for my father. Every minute of my childhood, I longed for my dad. I ached for him. He was my world. I remember getting out of school and "running away" to find him. I would wander the streets yelling his name until nine or ten o'clock at night. I was six years old. My useless search would end with me still craving my father's love and attention.

I don't know why I searched so hard for my dad. Fact is, he had an explosive temper. Everyone knew he was violent and crazy, and I was often on the wrong end of his fists. When I was three years old, he handed me a gun and told me to shoot the man across the table who had just beaten him in a game of dominos. Crazy times, just crazy. Besides being angry and violent, he was downright mean. One Christmas the church came around and gave our family bikes. Mine was a Huffy. I loved that bike. Two days later my dad gathered them all up and sent them to his children in Haiti. That was just wrong. Still, my dad was my everything.

Oh, there are some yellow lights! It will be good to get out of this drizzle.

Maybe the bond we shared was just on my side. Maybe I needed him more than he needed me.

What's that? The bus says, "Not in Service." Just like my dad.

I found plenty of dads on the streets, but they were only substitutes, fill-ins, and counterfeits. Using me to further their own plans, they taught me what a man is, how he acts, and what he does to hustle to survive. In the hierarchy of gang members, Willican was my up-line. I was in second grade, and he was in fifth. He taught me how to steal bikes to supply to the older gang members and how to fight with the Spanish kids. He drilled two important lessons into me: know your provider and know your enemy.

My cousin, Rick, was several levels up from Willican. Rick was cool. He was a fast, flashy drug dealer, and he always had a quick answer for everyone. He was a wise guy I could count on for a steady stream of amazing advice. It's kind of funny when I remember that his most consistent advice to me was not to be like him. That made me mad because he was all I wanted to be. I watched him and the other older kids, and I tried to imitate everything they did or said. There was no time to play games with kids my own age. Without a father, I needed to be a man quick.

Yellow lights are coming closer. Is this it? The #18 . . . yes! And it is in service. My wait is over. My bus is here. Time to get out of this rain, get moving on.

As I find a seat, I check my backpack for my paper. I won't have long after work to get to class. Good, it's not wet. I'll be able to turn it in. After working the night shift, I can't always understand what the professor is talking about so I want to make sure I turn in my homework. As I settle into my seat, I think of the ways God has provided some really great people in my life to carry me over some rough spots. Clyde, Gayle, and Julie were my big three.

My guardian ad litem, Clyde, faithfully showed up at all my meetings and always made sure I had the best care. Gayle, my therapist, was a wonderful listener and just a really supportive person.

And Julie was in a league of her own. She was my caseworker at the shelter, and we shared a special connection quickly. We spent endless hours together, and I thought of her as a mom. The feeling was mutual, and we talked about the day when she would adopt me. Months turned into years. Julie fell in love and got married. I guess her husband wasn't too crazy about the idea of a ready-made family because Julie stopped talking about adopting me. I don't think she'll ever understand what a crushing disappointment it was. I had waited for so long and come so close to being part of a family. All she said was that their plans had changed. I guess they wanted kids of their own instead.

In addition to the big three, there were others God used to show me "I am with you" and "I am for you." There was the foster family who took me across the street to a church. It was there that Jesus, once again, made it clear that I belonged to Him. Over the last year it has been the people at 4KIDS who have become my real family. Mr. Ken and Ms. Jeanette are like the parents I never had. My roommates—Quincy, Pat, and Hugo—are my brothers.

This new family of mine is always challenging me to grow as a leader. They encouraged me to go on an overseas outreach trip to work with orphans. Something life-changing happened when I went there. We took some kids from a local orphanage to the beach. When we were all playing in the waves, I heard someone yelling for help. One of the kids from the trip had sliced open his foot on some coral. Everyone was just standing there watching him bleed. I grabbed him and carried him to the car so that he could get to the hospital.

Everyone said I was a hero.

It felt good to have him holding onto my neck and to know that I was strong enough to help him. Someone was counting on me. Someone needed me.

All my life I've been angry for what I didn't have. It felt like everyone used me, and I thought the world owed me something. I still don't have it all straight, but I think God wants me to work with abandoned kids. I guess because I know how they feel. During that trip I realized I could make a difference in someone else's life.

> *"Now approaching Plantation General Hospital and Broward Boulevard with transfers to Route 22. Please refer to appropriate timetable for transfer times to connecting routes."*

Well, here I am at work. Oh, good, I'm early, and I didn't even get too wet. I'd better get in there. Kids are probably waiting for me. You could say I've come full circle. I'm now the one the kids see when the cops bring them in. After all the times I was brought here as a kid, now I walk through as a staff worker.

> *Lord, may I be used by You to comfort Your children tonight. Help me make a difference to a child who is waiting.*

ONE PERSON

No man makes a greater mistake than he who does nothing because he knows it is not everything.
—Edmund Burke

Maybe you've heard this story before. A young boy walking along the beach throws a starfish back into the ocean. An older man approaches the boy and asks him what he is doing. The young boy replies that he is saving starfish brought in by the tide. The older man looks up the beach and sees thousands of starfish and asks what possible difference this effort could make. The young boy smiles as he throws another starfish back into the surf, and says, "It matters to this one."

We all have the power to make a difference for one person. Our seemingly insignificant impact on a problem can have great impact on a single individual. But I believe this story contains a veiled, more dominant message. It is the inspiration of the one factor. One boy throwing back a starfish can inspire thousands to do the same. Small becomes big. One becomes thousands . . .

MY STORY

It matters to this one.
—A boy

Ever since I was a kid, I've known how to make money. Lemonade stands. Mowing lawns. Saving every penny. In college, it seemed only natural to major in finance. As with most people, I prayed very little about the career path I had chosen. I just pursued what I was good at. The summer after my sophomore year, I volunteered at a children's home in Indiana.

That's where I met Brian. Brian was kind of ordinary—an average twelve-year-old, nothing to signal that he would change my life forever. Brian had been assigned to help me cut the hedges lining the property. It was a hot day, and there were a lot of hedges. But things were going well, and I figured we would be done in a few hours. Another task successfully accomplished, until Brian asked me a question.

"Hey, Doug, have you ever tried to kill yourself?"

I chuckled, not even bothering to look over my shoulder, as I said no. I knew he had to be joking.

You know when silence is loud?

Brian wasn't laughing.

I put the hedge clippers down and looked at Brian. His face told me this was no joke. Then he told me his story. The hedges took much longer than I had planned.

The rest of my summer was different from that point. Even after I got home, my college classes left me feeling empty and dissatisfied. Making the numbers work just didn't cut it for me. I knew I wanted to work with kids—kids that people had forgotten about, kids like Brian.

A few weeks later I changed my major to education. Like a pool ball careening around the table, one conversation stopped me and sent me spinning off in a totally new direction. It led to subsequent conversations and exposed me to people and experiences that kept moving me in a direction.

For me, that conversation with Brian changed everything.

You're reading this book because of Brian, and he doesn't know any of this. The one factor works like that. Our view of the impact we have in others' lives, even if we notice it, is so limited. We can never track all the lives that one will inspire. Brian's life is living proof—his one has impacted thousands, and the number is growing every day.

FATHER OF THE YEAR

Father to the fatherless, defender of widows—this is God, whose dwelling is holy. God places the lonely in families . . . [8]
—David, King of Israel

When we opened our first home, KidsPlace, we didn't know much except that we wanted to help kids. We knew we needed houseparents, but we didn't have an HR department and weren't organized enough to have a sophisticated recruitment strategy (some things haven't changed). I just prayed and looked around, and there were Mark and Susan. They loved kids, though they didn't have any, and they possessed the most important quality to be a candidate—they were available.

No running water. The only bathroom, a small metal bucket in the corner. Rats coming and going as they please. Rancid odor.

Third-world poverty?

For eight-year-old Scott and his sister, Taneisha, this was first-world reality. Abandoned by their parents, they were passed from relative to relative until they landed with an uncle. Left to themselves, their living conditions rapidly deteriorated.

An anonymous tip alerted authorities to Scott and Taneisha's living conditions, and within hours they were rescued from their deplorable surroundings and thrust into foster care. Scott and Taneisha were brought to KidsPlace, a shelter designed to keep sibling groups together, until a foster family could be found to take them both.

Mark and Susan were their houseparents. Mark was a firefighter; Susan, a dental hygienist. They wanted to make a difference in children's lives, so they had committed to serving for two years at KidsPlace.

Within weeks of Scott's arrival, Mark recognized the challenge ahead. Scott was a handful. His lack of focus, coupled with his insatiable chatter, would drive even the most patient parent to the breaking point. The other children in the house were often victims of Scott's rage as he expressed himself through provoking, screaming, and hitting. Turmoil and Scott just seemed to go hand-in-hand. Mark occasionally glimpsed a softer side to Scott, even though he usually defaulted to destructive interactions with others. Scott seemed resigned to live the life of a victim, blaming everyone else for his problems.

Mark and Susan prayed for wisdom to help Scott find the stability and security he craved. Little by little, changes in Scott became noticeable as his heart opened to them. His behavior began to improve, and he sought out Mark's advice and approval. The tight bond between the two was apparent to even the most casual observer. Then one day the call came; a foster family had been found. A more permanent home was ready for Scott and Taneisha. With a combination of joy and grief, Mark helped Scott pack his things and vowed to keep in touch.

Unfortunately, once Scott left Mark's daily influence, he quickly regressed into his former patterns of anger—and two subsequent foster placements broke down from the strain.

During the same year, Mark and Susan moved from the shelter into their own home, having fulfilled their commitment as houseparents. Although their hearts and prayers would always be with Scott, Taneisha, and the other fifty-six foster children they had grown to love, they believed their service in foster care was complete. They were looking forward to a season of rest—until receiving the news that Scott and Taneisha were going to be split up in their next foster placement.

Separation would be devastating. Mark and Susan began to pray for God to provide a family to take both children. God answered. A few days later, Scott and Taneisha moved into Mark and Susan's new home.

Rest would have to wait.

Almost immediately, Scott's downward spiral experienced an upturn. Anger waned, grades improved, and interest in spiritual things re-awakened. His relationship with Mark seemed to pick up where it had left off. One day their conversation turned to the love of God. For the first time in his life, Scott seemed to grasp that God was his Father and had been there all along. Together they read Psalm 68:6 (NLT): God places the lonely in families . . . Scott's experience with Mark had become a window to God's provision.

That spring Scott was given a school assignment to write an essay about his father. Though he knew his birth father, Scott chose to write about Mark. The essay was entered in the 2004 Florida Father of the Year contest sponsored by the National Center for Fathering. Out of 15,000 essays, Scott's essay, "What My Father Means to Me," won first place.

"WHAT MY FATHER MEANS TO ME"

My father makes me feel like he's my real father even though he's my foster dad. His name is Mark, and he is a firefighter. He makes me feel safe when he's around. When he's at work, I still get to talk to him and sometimes we visit him. I can't wait until he comes home because he works for twenty-four hours, and I miss him when he's gone.

When I first came to live with Mr. Mark and Mrs. Susan, I was having hard times at school. When I had a bad day, he took the time to listen and understand how I felt. He helped me show more self-control by teaching me from the Bible. I even got student of the week. My teacher says that I'm the most improved student that she ever had in her whole five years of being a teacher. Now, I'm trying to get on the honor roll. Almost every day, he has me journal so he can know how to help me not make the same mistakes again. This shows me that he really cares about me. I feel special when I'm with him.

A couple of times I went with my dad to help him work on a house that he was fixing up. We left my sister and mother at home. It was just the guys hanging out together. He let me pull the brick out and put the sealer on the new patio. I caught a snake that was twelve inches. It was lots of fun helping my dad and finding the snake.

Spending more time with my dad makes me feel really special to him. I don't care what we do as long as we are together.

ANGEL

**Celebrities don't make the difference in society.
The little platoons of ordinary people living extraordinary lives do.
—Chuck Colson**

"You can't save every kid."

You've probably heard this truism more than once. I don't know about you, but that phrase can really rip me off. It gives me an excuse not to do anything at all because I can't do everything. When I start to get that sinking feeling that I can't possibly change a situation, I remember Maurice and Angel.

Maurice came home from school and reached for the front door. Locked again. He sat down on the front porch and waited. And waited and waited.

Maurice was used to waiting.

As dusk approached, a social worker turned into the gravel driveway. His mom was in the hospital again. She had another seizure. With no family around, Maurice would spend another couple nights in foster care until his mom got better.

Maurice was eight years old and this was his routine.

Uncertainty and instability were a part of life. The routine continued until he stayed at our house one night. My wife and I were respite foster parents, taking in kids for short amounts of time. When I heard Maurice's story, something didn't match. Maurice seemed like a happy-go-lucky kid without a care in the world, but his eager-to-please smile belied his tenuous situation. No eight-year-old should live like Maurice was living. He needed something more . . . but I was way over committed.

Our church has a mentoring program that provides Big Brothers for fatherless kids. I made sure Maurice's name made it to the top of the list. A few weeks later a mentor came forward; his name was Angel.

The first year Angel signed a one-year contract to be Maurice's mentor and meet with him once a week. They spent Saturdays hanging out, playing football, and going to church. After the first year they forgot to re-sign the contract, committing to another year. Families don't need contracts. Maurice still needed a place to sleep many nights, but now there was no question where he would be staying. Seven years later Maurice is part of the family.

Angel knows that some of the most important things they talk about are often the hardest for Maurice to put into words. After all these years, Angel knows Maurice so well that he can read through the silence. Like the time Angel asked how football practice was going and Maurice told him it hadn't started. Angel knew he needed to take Maurice to Wal-Mart to get cleats so that the coach would allow him to practice. Or the time Maurice's phone number was disconnected, Angel knew he needed to contact the phone company to work out a payment schedule for Maurice. That's what mentors are for—understanding the things you don't say as easily as those that you do say.

When Angel fell in love with Carla, he introduced her to Maurice. She knew he was part of the deal. After they were married for a few years, Angel and Carla had a son, Julian. Now when Maurice spends the night, you'll find him and Julian up early on Saturday mornings sprawled on the floor watching cartoons together, both convulsing in laughter.

Angel has taught Maurice many life lessons, the kinds of lessons a father passes on to his son—how to face your fears on the first day of middle school, how to avoid fights by watching your mouth, and the value of studying and persevering through those difficult days of high school.

Many of these life lessons were taught by example. When Maurice got his first paycheck from his first job, he saved ten percent and gave away ten percent because that's what Angel does.

And Maurice has taught Angel and Carla a few lessons of his own. They now know what life is like for kids who don't have a stable family—kids who don't eat dinner around a table, have a curfew, or have someone to help out with schoolwork. They have gained insight into a learning disability that allows a young man to memorize ten years of sports stats and yet struggle in math class. They have learned that the power of persuasion is a survival skill for a ten-year-old who regularly needs to call the power company and ask for a little more time before the electricity is cut off.

Knowing Maurice makes Angel and Carla want to be foster parents. Knowing Angel and Carla makes Maurice want to get married and have children of his own some day. And that's why Angels are important.

> *I chatted with Angel, Carla, and Maurice in church a few weeks back and just smiled as I walked away. Seven years ago I didn't have the time to invest in Maurice, but that didn't mean I was powerless. I linked one person to another and got out of the way. The one factor did the rest.*

THE PROMISE

I will not leave you as orphans; I will come to you.[9]
—Jesus

Juan set out to prove that no one could ever hurt him like his father had . . . ever again. He was determined to protect himself by proving he was unlovable. But a housedad, Andre, promised to prove just the opposite, and his love finally broke through. Sometimes kids just need to know that you're in it for the long haul; you're in it forever.

Juan was eight years old the day his dad left him. His dad was on another crack binge, and this time he took his son with him to make the buy. Juan vividly remembers every detail of the crack house, but especially the last words his dad ever said to him:

"I'll be right back!"

And then he was gone.

Four days later Juan was picked up from the crack house and placed into protective custody. With no parent to care for him, Juan was an orphan.

Although he found a home with an aunt and uncle, Juan determined never to get close to anyone again. He could never allow someone to hurt him that deeply again. He was placed in a special school for kids with behavior problems, where he assumed the role of a tough guy. Profanity, arguments, fights, and disrespect all trailed closely behind Juan. His anger made him so irrational that on the drive home from school with his uncle one day, he jumped out of a moving car and ran away.

Juan was picked up by police the next day and placed in foster care. That's the day Juan met Andre. Andre was the new house dad at Guys-Place, a home for teenage boys. Juan made it clear to his caseworker and Andre that he did not want to be there, and he promised to make it difficult for everyone. He kept his promise. Andre, an unassuming man of great patience, also made a promise to himself and to God: He would not give up on Juan. Ever.

Juan kept his promise.

Andre kept his promise.

Through consistency, discipline, and love, Andre endured all that Juan could dish out. And then one day the turning point came. Andre was at Juan's school to talk to the principal because Juan had been suspended again. In the middle of the discussion between Juan, the principal, and Andre, Andre excused himself to walk outside and collect his thoughts. Juan thought he was leaving him and instinctively cried out, "Don't leave me! I want to go home with you!"

Uncontrollable sobbing followed Juan's frantic cry. The walls Juan had built around his heart came crashing down. Andre had broken through.

It would make a perfect ending to say that everything was better after that, and they all lived happily ever after—but like most real stories, the struggle continues. This is not a fairy tale. It is what Andre would describe as a God Story, one where you know it was more than the sum of the parts that led to this breakthrough, and the ones to follow.

Juan set out to prove that no one would ever hurt him like his father, ever again. He was determined to protect himself by proving he was unlovable. Andre promised to prove the opposite, and his love finally broke through. Juan would say he changed because Andre outlasted him. If you ask Andre, he would tell you he kept the weightier promise.

THE GRAND JURY
AND THE NURSING HOME

Whoever finds his life will lose it,
and whoever loses his life for my sake will find it.[10]
—Jesus

I'm often asked to give talks about what people can do for chil-
dren in foster care. I provide facts about foster care and the
faces behind those facts, and people are usually eager to help.
How could you not want to help a child who is suffering be-
cause of the sins of others? But too often enthusiasm dwindles
because these kids need more than charity. They need us—an
investment of our time to help them overcome their pasts and
develop strength to move forward. They need our lives so they
can recover some of theirs.

"Most of the children in foster care are spoiled..." As the words left my
mouth, side-chatter abruptly stopped as eyes widened and refocused in
disbelief. I knew I had some explaining to do.

The grand jury was convening on the issue of foster care, and I had been
called to testify about my experiences working within the system. For several weeks, this group of ordinary citizens had heard testimony from children who had been treated more like animals than children. Horrific
abuse. Things that would make you sick.

Children in foster care spoiled? I could see the panel struggling with the idea. I did my best to explain. Children suffer trauma. People feel sorry for their suffering and want to make it all better. So they give them things to produce a smile (and ease their own sense of guilt). That's why every Christmas foster children are inundated with gifts. But by January the smiles are gone—because things do not heal emotional and spiritual pain. Genuine healing takes a lot more time and effort.

Too often we don't think through what we are doing. In an effort to make up for the past, we give in to their wishes. Let children stay up late: they've been through so much. No vegetables: they don't like them. Extra credit for everything: they aren't capable of the same effort as other children.

These well-intentioned attempts deny children the very structure and boundaries they need to mature. They stunt the growth process. Bottom line: traumatized children need compassion more than sympathy.

Sympathy feels sorry; compassion suffers with.

Sympathy is a quick fix; compassion is the journey.

Sympathy creates entitlement; compassion fosters personal responsibility.

Sympathy keeps a child looking back; compassion moves a child forward.

Compassion refuses to allow a child's past to define the future. Through the hugs and tears, difficult questions, and sleepless nights, compassion whispers that a child's past can be the very thing God uses to bring redemption. Pain provides insight. When a child can serve another person in spite of personal pain, his pain gains purpose. The experience becomes the raw material God uses.

God wastes nothing.

Here is the paradox: Healing comes through serving others more than focusing on meeting your own needs. By serving others you help yourself.

When I met Lou, he was big on sympathy. A great guy, anxious to help. His heart was as big as the Montana sky. He saw the kids in the shelter and wanted to do something to ease their pain, so he showed up faithfully every week and brought them candy. It made him feel really good inside.

After a few weeks Lou realized that the kids had started demanding more stuff. They expected it. They felt entitled to it. And when it wasn't what they expected, the complaining started. That is where most volunteers leave in frustration, mumbling about ungrateful kids. But not Lou. Lou was willing to re-think his approach and pursue something that would bring about a genuine change. And then he had a strange and wonderful idea.

After a lot of legwork, phone calls, and paperwork, he arranged to take a van full of foster kids to a home for elderly people. He told the kids they were going to serve other people in need. When they arrived, the kids stood around looking at each other, but after a few initial awkward moments, they started passing out quilts. They had a few conversations. The eyes of the lonely, weak, and vulnerable residents had a mysterious effect.

There was a connection.

By the end of the afternoon, the kids were singing songs and a few even prayed with their new friends. Sometime that afternoon a transformation took place. Complaining turned into gratitude. Whining turned into joy. The most difficult kids were racing from person to person, competing like a relay team to meet the needs of those worse off than themselves. In serving the lonely, these "victims" discovered how much they had to offer. And it felt really good.

That Saturday afternoon, far from the grand jury's view, a handful of foster children took a step toward their own healing by reaching out to others. They had regained their identity, not as powerless victims, but as young people with much to offer the world. Their pasts had provided them insight into suffering that most kids will never know.

All because one man named Lou went the extra mile to give the gift of compassion. Compassion is the gift money can't buy. It is the gift that lasts. Lou gave them that gift . . . and they gave it away.

METAMORPHOSIS

**You begin saving the world by saving one man at a time,
all else is grandiose romanticism or politics.
—Charles Bukowski**

*I love before and after pictures. I remember our first house and
all the work my wife, Suzanne, and I put into it. Looking at it
now, it's hard to believe it's the same house. But my favorite before and after picture is not of a house. It's a picture in my office of a young woman whose eyes are so full of light, you could
get lost in them. But it wasn't always like that for Gabrielle.*

Darkness enveloped Gabrielle. Her hair, her clothes, her very spirit were
cloaked in darkness. Her despair was so deep she seemed to extinguish
whatever joy was in a room.

Gabrielle and her brother were raised by a mother addicted to drugs
and an avid follower of witchcraft. For as long as she could remember,
Gabrielle had played the role of caregiver, responsible for scrounging for
food and a place to live. Her mother had taken her out of school after first
grade with some vague reference to home schooling, but in reality
Gabrielle received no formal education for the next ten years. Her days
were filled with doing whatever she could to survive while her mother and
brother spiraled downward into their addictions.

This cycle of neglect continued until Gabrielle turned sixteen. A few weeks after her birthday, her mother handed her a faded twenty-dollar bill and told her to find somewhere else to live. Gabrielle was accustomed to not knowing where she and her family were going to live from week to week, but at least they had been together. Now, at age sixteen, Gabrielle was cut off. She was completely on her own.

With no relatives or friends to turn to, Gabrielle did the only thing she could think of—she called the child-abuse hotline. After years of pretending that everything was okay, she summoned the courage to blurt out, "I've been abandoned. I need someone to take care of me!"

Little did she know, that one phone call would mark the beginning of her metamorphosis.

Gabrielle was quickly picked up by police and taken to SafePlace. She stood in the doorway, cloaked in black, clutching her books on witchcraft. The volunteer who welcomed her remembers Gabrielle's eyes reflecting only abject despair. She silently pleaded with God to pierce the darkness and surround Gabrielle with His people.

One desperate prayer. And God's answer was swift.

There was an opening at GirlsPlace, a home for teenage girls. When Gabrielle arrived, houseparents Don and Loretta poured their love and kindness on her, but Gabrielle struggled to accept it. She would say to Loretta, "You people are freakishly nice." She fended off any physical gesture of affection, even a simple hug. When she felt threatened, even by expressions of love, Gabrielle would cope with the pain by cutting herself. She daily battled with thoughts of inadequacy and suicide.

I remember the day she came into my office and showed me the still fresh wounds on her arms. That day, her dark thoughts grew so intense that she had to be hospitalized for her own protection. I secretly wondered, How much pain could be in one person's heart?

At every step in Gabrielle's journey, her new family continued to reach out to love her. Don and Loretta's love did not falter despite Gabrielle's sneaking out at night, habitual lying, and rejection of their love. Gabrielle had never seen this kind of unwavering commitment.

Deep within her heart, Gabrielle realized she was missing something. Her Wiccan beliefs had led her to despair. She needed a new faith—the kind of faith she had tested in Don and Loretta but wasn't able to break. She needed a Savior to take away the darkness inside her.

She opened her heart and something amazing happened inside Gabrielle. Light. Forgiveness. Healing. Hope.

Four years after placing that fateful call, the darkness that defined Gabrielle is gone. She now walks with a peace and confidence that only comes when your soul is reborn. Now when she enters a room, darkness flees. Her face is radiant. Those of us who know her best describe her in a single word: JOY!

A few months ago, when Gabrielle was in my office, I looked down at the scars on her arms. She followed my glance. It was one of those unspoken moments when we silently replayed that difficult day in my office a few years earlier. Gabrielle broke the silence, "I forget they're there," she said. "They seem like they are from another life. But you know, if I could get rid of them, I wouldn't—because they will always remind me of what God rescued me from."

Recently I interviewed Gabrielle before hundreds of pastors and leaders at a community breakfast. As she spoke of her experiences and the difficulty of her transformation, she broke down and began to weep. The room fell silent as I did my best to help her regain her composure. After a brief pause she shared something that gripped us all: "I'm not crying for me. I am crying for all the girls who didn't get the home I got. I am crying for them."

Gabrielle enrolled in high school after a nine-year absence and graduated within three years. She is attending a community college and plans to get her master's degree in social work. She volunteers each week teaching Sunday school at her church, offering her welcoming smile to everyone she meets. Last week I signed the paperwork for Gabrielle to be hired as a 4KIDS staff member, serving the kids she understands all too well.

ONE MOMENT

"Carpe diem"

I love to watch basketball, especially during the play-offs when the stakes are so high. If you are a sports fan, you know the power of one moment. It is a phenomenon we describe as a swing in momentum. One team can be dominating the other and then all of sudden . . . one play changes everything. In a game of a hundred plays, one has the power to turn the tide.

This is one of the reasons we love a good movie. Every good movie has that moment when the tide turns—an act of courage, a change of mind, a word of inspiration, or an act of sacrifice. From that moment everything is different. The hair on your arms stands up. A chill runs through your body. Your eyes well up.

We react this way because our lives are a lot like that. You are just about to give up, but in one moment something tips the scale and provides enough inspiration to accomplish what you never thought you could.

Think about where you are in your life right now.

How did you get there?

Trace back to the decisions that led you to where you live, what you do, who you spend time with. If you keep going back, all these can be traced to a fork in your road where you had to make a difficult decision. That choice led to a series of choices that brought you to where you are now. And something at that fork swayed you to choose the road you're on now. If you had chosen the other path, your life would be completely different (if you are an over-thinker, you've spent hours analyzing this). The power of that one moment has changed your life forever.

One moment in time has that power.

I wonder how many of these moments I miss in a day. I'm so busy. Most days I'm just thinking about all my own stuff, my own issues, simply trying to get through life. I'm afraid I treat many moments of great potential too casually, as if they will always be there, as if they can be re-played. But I am learning that if moments aren't seized, they are often lost forever.

The one factor can take a seemingly inconsequential moment and reveal its power. That power can usually only be seen in retrospect. Which is why we miss so many of them.

GRADUATION DAY

Rejoice with those who rejoice . . . [11]
—Paul, the Apostle

Dysfunctional families rarely celebrate anything. We've met eight-year-olds who have never celebrated a birthday and sixteen-year-olds who have never decorated a Christmas tree. This is one of the reasons we work so hard to create moments of celebration for the kids in our care.

Today is a reason to celebrate. Staff members carefully set out platters overflowing with homemade specialties. Others huddle in the corner feverishly signing cards of congratulations. This is no ordinary Thursday staff meeting. Today we honor the graduates of the class of 2006. Today each one will be "roasted and honored." This cherished tradition provides the moments of laughter and words of empowerment that each graduate will need to draw from in the future. Few people expected these eight young men and women to graduate, but the handful that did are here to celebrate.

Each young person's journey to this celebration was as diverse as the group itself. Kim experienced a crisis pregnancy and dropped out of school. Pat spent his teenage years in a group home for difficult boys.

Gabrielle had been out of school for a decade. Thomas spent most of his life in foster care. With so many good reasons to quit, each one had somehow found the courage and endurance to press on.

One by one the graduates stand in front of the room and listen while staff members and foster parents share the memories marking their journeys through life. They speak about character forged through difficulties, about when the temptation to quit seemed almost irresistible. Each story yields its own nostalgic smiles and nods of recognition.

And then it is time for the graduates to speak.

Kim is first. She walks to the front slowly and quietly. She speaks barely above a whisper as she announces the dreams she has for her newborn son, Jonathan, and the hope of how she can provide for him.

Mez walks to the front next, wearing a proud smile. You can see the sense of accomplishment all over his face, a feeling he has seldom experienced in life. For all the times people had told him he could never become anything, this is his day to prove them wrong.

Thomas thanks all the people who made this day possible for him. He is especially excited as he talks about his earning potential. He offers a wry smile as he promises to not forget the "little people" when he gets rich.

Pat grins from ear to ear as he waits for his name to be called. He doesn't seem to mind being last as he swaggers forward to the chant "bling-bling," in recognition of his diamond-stud earrings. He stands tall and proud behind the podium as he rattles off an Academy-Award-like tribute to everyone who contributed to this day. Pat's final words remind the staff of the eternal significance of their work. "Here at 4KIDS, I found Jesus," he concludes. His smile threatens to overtake his face.

The ceremony closes as the staff gathers around the graduates and prays for them. There are prayers of gratitude and affirmation, prayers for their future—that God will again meet them in their moments of need, filling them with courage and hope. The bond of love in the room is palpable.

As the staff and graduates wipe away their tears and offer parting hugs, the room slowly clears. Some overhear another graduate, Hugo, say, "I don't call this a program; I call this a family."

Graduation Day 2006 was supposed to be an event we created to honor and inspire kids who would need this memory as a reference point in life. But we significantly underestimated the effect this moment would have on us. Our team worked hard to create an atmosphere of honor for the graduates, but we were the ones who were truly honored. For many of us it was the highlight of the year—one moment that revived us like a cold drink of water in the desert. In a vocation littered with sorrow and heartache, we got a taste of the fruit of our labor. It energized each one of us for the class of 2007, 2008, 2009 . . .

THE FUNERAL

. . . mourn with those who mourn.[12]
—Paul, the Apostle

Things happen in life that you just don't expect. And when the right response is not in the instruction manual, sometimes you have to make it up along the way. A ten-year-old boy needed closure after his mother died, and more importantly, he needed to know who was going to stand with him as he faced an uncertain future.

Vashan slowly made his way into the chapel. Dressed in his Sunday best, he awkwardly slid into the pew next to his foster dad, clutching a memorial program with a washed-out picture of his mother—the only reminder he had of her. At thirty-five she had died of AIDS, a virtual stranger to her son.

Vashan grew up in a home filled with poverty, abuse, and neglect. When teachers and neighbors discovered the condition of the children who lived in the house, they contacted the police, who removed the children. Vashan and his sister were placed in an emergency shelter, while relatives took in his cousins. Eventually, Vashan's sister found a home with an aunt, leaving

Vashan alone in foster care. Vashan was a tough sell for any family. He was big for his age with an IQ well below average. Because of his circumstances, he lacked the social skills of most ten-year-olds, and he still wet the bed at night.

As the service started, Vashan adjusted his borrowed tie and slouched forward, resting his chin in his hand. The pastor spoke about God's purposes in his mom's life and the hope Vashan could have for his future. Vashan's former housedad spoke next of the man of character Vashan was becoming and how proud his mom would be to see him now. Then it was his counselor's turn to speak of Vashan's many gifts and how everyone who knew him loved him. A mentor walked to the podium and recounted the fun they'd had together throwing a football around on Saturdays.

Finally, it was time for Vashan's foster dad to speak. He paused for what seemed like an eternity and then, looking directly into Vashan's eyes, he shared a promise: "God will never leave you or forsake you . . . and neither will I."

What made this funeral unusual was not that Vashan was in foster care or that his mom had died at such a young age. What made it so unusual was that Vashan was the only family member who attended this service. None of his brothers or sisters, aunts or uncles, or grandparents were there for him to share his grief. The family had attended his mother's funeral a few weeks earlier, but he had not been invited. He was still the black sheep of the family.

Tears streaked down Vashan's face and the faces of all those seated in the small chapel. Vashan cried for his mother.

Everyone else cried for Vashan.

As the service ended, Vashan sat in the pew, quiet and reflective. His eyes slowly scanned the faces surrounding him. For each of the eight who attended the memorial service, it was a moment they would never forget. Never had so many emotions converged in one moment: pity and love, pathos and hope.

This memorial service wasn't for Vashan's mom. It was for one boy who needed help in saying goodbye to his mother. Vashan needed a family to help him do that.

As Vashan walked out of the chapel, he seemed more at ease. His eyes reflected a hope beaming from the eight people who organized this funeral, just for him.

"I DON'T THINK I HAVE A MOMMY ANYMORE"

. . . just as despair can come to one another only from other human beings,
hope, too, can be given to one only by other human beings.
—Elie Wiesel

Holidays can be difficult for children in foster care. It's a time
when you are supposed to be with family to celebrate. What if
Mother's Day was approaching and all you could think about
was whether you'd ever see your mother again?

Cassandra arrived at KidsPlace—a scared little six-year-old, clutching
the hand of her social worker as they entered the house. This was her first
time in the foster care system, and it was Mother's Day weekend. The
scene in the dining room was joyous chaos as the children sheltered at
KidsPlace crowded around the dining room table intent on their projects.
Anxious hands darted out to grab the crayon that was just the right shade
of pink. Brows furrowed in concentration as children chose the right stick-
ers and judged the perfect amount of glitter on their way to creating the
perfect Mother's Day cards.

"Cassandra, we're glad to meet you! There's room for you right here," said
Mariah, a volunteer, as she motioned for Cassandra to join them at the table.
Cassandra stood perfectly still as tears of confusion and pain welled up in

her eyes. She looked at the crayons, construction paper, glue, and glitter. Mariah had to strain to catch Cassandra's barely audible words:

"I don't think I have a mommy anymore."

As Mariah looked into Cassandra's eyes, she glimpsed her unspoken entreaty, Why can't I be with my mommy?

That same question threatened to overwhelm Mariah every time she volunteered at KidsPlace. Somehow, the words came and Mariah quickly reassured Cassandra that she did still have a mommy who loved her. "If you don't want to make a card for your mommy, why don't you make one for your housemom, Lydia?" Mariah suggested.

In an instant Cassandra's tears stopped and a huge smile spread across her face. "Ok!" she replied as her slender fingers dipped into the glitter to begin the task of creating a big sunny happy face on the front of her card.

The next day Cassandra impatiently hopped from foot to foot as her new housemother, Lydia, opened up her very first Mother's Day card. Tears streamed down Lydia's face as she traced the childish scrawl, "hapy mohters day," and brushed her fingers over the glitter and clumps of glue. Three simple words unleashed a joy within Lydia's heart that she had never known she craved. In the midst of her own confusion and fear, Cassandra had unknowingly touched a hunger in her interim mom. Cassandra stood grinning and beaming with pride as she watched the tears course down Lydia's face faster than she could wipe them away.

It was not an accident that Lydia and Cassandra met that year. It was a perfect moment in time, orchestrated by God to meet the unspoken needs of Lydia and Cassandra. They didn't know how much they needed each other. The years have passed. Lydia now has a child of her own, and Cassandra has been reunited with her mother, but that was one Mother's Day neither will soon forget.

"WILL ANYBODY TAKE MY SON?"

Fear can hold you a prisoner. Hope can set you free.
—The Shawshank Redemption

My friend, Reuben, and I used to lead a Bible study in a juvenile lock-down facility once a week during our lunch break. We knew this was a forgotten group of kids, so we wanted to be there for them—talking, praying, and tackling whatever issues the young men would bring up in our discussions. Every one of the young men had a story, but there was one story we will never forget.

James was a prisoner. At fifteen, he had already been convicted of a string of felonies. Even in jail, James' uncontrollable anger erupted in fights with his peers and sometimes with staff members. A frequent visitor to solitary confinement, he was placed on medication and received counseling—but nothing seemed to change. James was out of control.

Bored and restless on a Wednesday afternoon, James decided to check out our weekly Bible study. Although James walked into the meeting appearing quiet and reserved, his orange jumpsuit told a different story; it was used only for the most aggressive inmates. James managed a few questions toward the end of the discussion, but we secretly doubted whether he would come back. To our surprise, James wandered into the following week's study. James quickly became a regular, attending every week.

Over the next several weeks, we recognized James as a study in contradictions. On one hand, he was incredibly insightful and articulate. He asked probing questions and easily grasped even the most complex ideas. He showed a lighter side, laughing and cracking jokes with the other boys. But James had a darker side. Cynical, sarcastic, and malicious, he could stifle the most transformational moments with a few well-chosen words or a provocative gesture. On any given Wednesday afternoon, we didn't know which James to expect. As soon as we felt James was making genuine progress, he would push us away through outright defiance. Several times we asked him to leave the group when his antagonistic behavior became too disruptive.

One day James didn't show up for Bible study. When I inquired about his absence, I discovered that he had been re-arrested within the jail for assaulting a guard. Reuben and I found out where he was being held and drove across town to visit him. We met with James in a plexi-glass holding cell. His mood was somber. After some small talk, James dropped his defenses and gave us a glimpse into his heart and mind. I have no idea why James chose to share with us that day. Maybe it was our persistence to pursue him. Maybe he was just tired of holding it all in. Whatever the reason, the story he told would be one that would live forever in my memory.

It started out as an all-too-familiar story: a father he never knew, a mom in over her head trying to raise two boys alone, drugs, bad relationships, evictions, arrests, poverty, and abuse. It was all a blur to James, except for one moment he played over and over again in his head.

When he was nine years old, his mother put him and his younger brother into a shopping cart and wheeled them down to the local church. As the service let out and the congregants streamed by her, she asked each family a shocking question,

"Will anybody take my sons?"

James' words slowed as he described the scene. His eyes reflected the bewildered hurt and betrayal he had felt as person after person looked into his dirty little face and then quickly turned away. His own mother didn't want him and neither did anyone else. He was a throwaway kid, a reject.

James sat across from us, his head hung low, his voice cracking from the strain. And then I saw something I had never seen from James before . . . tears. They slowly rolled down his face, and as they hit the concrete floor, they seemed to awaken James from his trance. Wiping them away, he continued his story.

The same scene was played out the next Sunday at a different church where a family agreed to take his brother. James' voice was flat and expressionless as he described watching his brother leave, not knowing if he would ever see him again. The next Sunday James and his mother were at yet another church with a similar plea,

"Will anybody take my son?"

A family agreed to take James. Finally the humiliation was over. James had a new family, but the damage was done.

He bounced from home to home because of his behavior, eventually ending up in foster care and ultimately jail.

Reuben and I sat in stunned silence. James had opened up his heart for the slightest moment, and a tidal wave of pain had crashed out. Trying to regain his composure, he cracked a crass joke and attempted to make small talk. I grabbed James' shoulder and looked him straight in his eyes. Although words seemed inadequate, I told James the truth: "Though my father and mother forsake me, the LORD will receive me."[13]

It was God's message for James, his brother, and all the children whose parents are unable or unwilling to care for them. Our eyes locked as he soaked in my words. Reuben and I prayed for him, and then we parted ways.

We walked out of the jail and silently drove back to work. How could this happen to a child? The words we offered seemed so puny and inadequate in the face of such a primal grief. Now it made sense why James was so angry and why he refused to be loved. His story had provided us the key to his paradoxical behavior. Who could question why he was so anxious to sabotage any conversation or relationship that threatened to penetrate his carefully constructed defenses?

James was in jail because he knew that if he were released, he had no place to go. No family. No friends. Nobody.

He was fifteen and totally alone in the world. A lost boy.

For James, life outside the detention center was scarier than life inside. Bars or no bars, his pain and fear kept him in prison.

We never saw James again. The next week when we went to visit, he was gone. He had assaulted another guard and was transferred to a facility out of the area.

As I write this, questions still race through my mind. Are there lost causes? Are there ones who are too far over the edge to be pulled back to safety? I can't always answer these questions, but I find great hope in the words I spoke to James that day.

As incomprehensible as it may seem, God knew that some parents would abandon their own children. But God is not shocked by our depravity; He makes provision for it. I find comfort in the fact that although I couldn't solve James' problem or take away the pain, I could offer him a brief glimpse into the unconditional love of God.

And I know that sometimes a simple truth in the right moment can make all the difference in the world.

THE CRISIS

Never let your head hang down.
Never give up and sit down and grieve. Find another way.
—Satchel Paige

Mom. Dad. I'm pregnant!

It's one of a parent's worst fears.

But Ray and Anne resolved to walk through the crisis with their daughter. And it made them wonder what would happen if a teenage girl did not have supportive parents. What would she do? And what they did twenty years ago is still changing lives to this day.

They established a home for pregnant girls called His Caring Place—a place where a family and a community walk through the crisis with young girls. Ray and Anne did not want to waste their experience. They took their crisis and made it a moment that has affected thousands. Twenty years later their decision caught up with one girl named Chloe.

Chloe was sixteen years old, pregnant, and in foster care. Abandoned by her parents, she sat at SafePlace and waited . . . and waited. It was a double shock—she never expected to be pregnant and never expected to have to face life all alone. It didn't take too long for Chloe to figure out that being a pregnant teenager in foster care severely limited the people willing to take her in.

After a few days at SafePlace, Chloe met a counselor from His Caring Place and was offered a place at one of their homes. Chloe gathered her few belongings and was taken to the house where she was greeted by Olga, the housemother. Olga was a single parent raising a teenager of her own. Chloe sensed that Olga knew what it was like to be all alone in the world; Chloe also recognized a quiet strength in Olga—a strength she knew she was lacking.

Over the next several days, Olga spoke to Chloe about her options. They talked about the challenges of raising a child with little or no support system. Chloe seemed overwhelmed by the prospect of raising a child, so Olga asked, "Have you ever considered placing your baby with an adoptive family?"

Olga waited as Chloe sat silently contemplated the question. Then slowly and quietly, Chloe began to speak, her voice cracking with emotion.

"I want a family to adopt me," Chloe told Olga.

Even though Chloe was old enough to be a mother, she had not outgrown her own need for a family. Chloe wanted what we all want—to belong, to know that no matter what happens, someone will always be at the kitchen table ready to talk.

Twenty years earlier, Ray and Anne chose to allow their crisis to be a catalyst, one they never anticipated would affect so many, one that provided a desperately needed family for one girl named Chloe when she needed it most.

Sometimes the moments you dread most in life become the greatest opportunities. The one factor reminds us that a crisis doesn't have to be in vain. Instead, it can be a moment pregnant with potential.

ONE IDEA

If at first, the idea is not absurd, then there is no hope for it.
—Albert Einstein

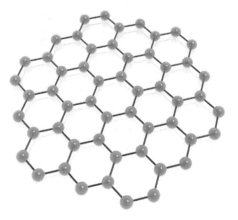

I don't remember much from middle school (except being turned down for the eighth-grade dance by Stacy Anderson), but one thing I remember from middle-school science class is a picture of a ball at the top of a hill. It was just sitting there. The teacher explained that this represented potential energy. All this pent up energy, all this possible momentum doing nothing. Power resting. But then there was another picture next to it. A picture of the ball rolling down a hill. Kinetic energy.

Something caused that ball to start moving.

Usually it is one thing that starts the ball rolling. Now it is kinetic. In motion, — gathering momentum all on its own.

Ideas are like that. For most of us, they lay dormant at the top of a hill somewhere. They are great ideas with so much potential, but they don't get any traction. We let them sit up there, and then we complain when one of these simple ideas make someone else a millionaire. (Maybe you watch infomercials just to see who stole your ideas.) One simple idea can create momentum that changes the very way we live life. We call this an idea whose time has come.

Consider the invention of the cell phone. Now think of all the corresponding technological advances that have grown from a simple portable communication device. The ball has been nudged and is rolling faster every day.

I've learned a lot about the one factor from people who dared to strike out into uncharted territory. Their courage, determination, and boldness may fly in the face of conventional wisdom, but don't most great ideas? Sometimes the idea is so simple and obvious we underestimate its power. And then we have to get out of the way of the tumbling rocks. Avalanche!

GOD SPEAKS

Let's talk.
—GOD

You've probably seen the billboards along the highway—all black background, white lettering, a simple message, an unexpected author.

> *Keep using my name in vain,*
> *I'll make rush hour longer.*
> *—GOD*

> *I love you. I love you. I love you.*
> *—GOD*

When I first saw them, I thought, "What a great idea!" Creative, funny, challenging, something to make everybody think. The idea for these billboards started in 1998 with a few people in an office brainstorming ideas on how to get people to think about God and His love for them.

What about placing simple, easy-to-read messages in a place everyone could see? What type of location would provide repetitive moments of undivided attention? How about putting the messages on billboards? Everyone sits in traffic at some point. The ball was nudged and started to roll.

An advertising agency was hired and eighteen billboards were set to run in South Florida for three months. Then a billboard company called and donated a few more. Then a national advertising company picked up on the idea. In a few months more than ten thousand donated billboards in more than two hundred cities across America were making people think about God.

Books, T-shirts, a website, thousands of dollars generated. No one expected to make any money. What could they do with it? One idea led to another. Another ball started rolling. How about a home for foster kids? Wouldn't God love that?

In 2002 a four-bedroom house was purchased with the proceeds from the GodSpeaks campaign. That home, KidsPlace, was no ordinary emergency shelter. It was a model of what a shelter could be—a home where brothers and sisters wouldn't be split up, a home in a regular neighborhood with parents, a backyard, and a pool.

The ball was getting bigger, rolling faster, and spinning off other balls. This innovation led to four more family-style shelters. The state system saw the effectiveness of these homes and shifted its paradigm to encourage smaller, more intimate homes for foster children rather than large institutional housing.

One simple idea, another idea, a dozen more. Avalanche. Thousands of lives forever changed. This is the one factor making the small, big.

Had any good ideas lately?

TAYLOR'S CLOSET

There is one thing stronger than all the armies in the world,
and that is an idea whose time has come.
—Victor Hugo

Imagine what it would be like to be going through a tough time,
taken from your parents, attending a new school, and feeling
like you are drawing negative attention to yourself because you
are a foster child. School is brutal enough without the teasing
that accompanies the donated, out-of-style, worn clothes most
foster children wear.

Lindsay loves to shop. She loves the way trying on a new outfit makes
her feel and knows that buying clothes is more about identity than neces-
sity. One day Lindsay read about the difficult journey that awaited girls
her age in foster care. She began to wonder what she could do to help.

A few months later while on a summer vacation, she had a crazy idea
to match her love of clothes with this need. She could start a clothing store,
a boutique of designer clothes, where girls in foster care could shop for
free.

It could be run by kids, for kids.

She could call her friends and start collecting clothes right away—only the best clothes, name brands, the kind of clothes all her friends wore. She talked with her parents, and they encouraged her to think it through. Where would the clothes be stored? How would she get the word out to girls in need? Who would run this store? Where would the money come from to get it set up?

Undeterred, she began to talk to people and ask questions until she was able to write her vision down on paper. That's when I met Lindsay. She scheduled an appointment, and flanked by her parents, she pitched her idea to me. As I listened to Lindsay, I knew her parents were in big trouble. This was clearly an idea whose time had come. As a first step, I suggested a Christmas outreach where we would arrange for a dozen girls in foster care to shop through her inventory.

Lindsay started in her own closet, and then talked to all her friends. Before long, her family's dining room table was overflowing with clothes. The Christmas event was a great success, and it was there that she met Tom whose daughter, Rachael, works for a retail design company. Rachael heard about the concept from her dad and talked to her boss, who, in turn, had Lindsay present her idea to the entire staff at their corporate headquarters. I can't help but smile when I think of this spunky fourteen-year-old girl making her presentation in a corporate boardroom.

Taylor's Closet was born. Individuals, corporations, and nonprofits rushed to be a part. We provided the space, and Rachael's company paid for the $50,000 build-out. Clothing manufacturers donated designer clothes by the pallet. Then local media picked up the story. National media soon followed: ABC World News Tonight, NPR, Geraldo at Large. The website received thirty thousand hits from fifty-five countries. Hundreds of e-mails poured in inquiring how to start a similar store in communities across the country. And all without a single dollar spent on advertising,

Lindsay's simple idea had caught fire.

Today when you walk into Taylor's Closet, you will see that Lindsay's vision has become a reality. Brand-new and gently used name-brand styles from top designers like Roxy and Burberry dangle from wooden hangers against bright orange and purple walls. You will see Lindsay and her friends laughing and joking behind the counter. They are not much different than your average teenagers, except that they are on a mission. Every girl who walks through the doors will receive one-on-one attention, not just to fit and accessorize the clothes, but also to experience the words set high on the shelves. Hope. Love. Reminders that this store is providing more than just another outfit.

Lindsay's mom describes it best: "It's all bigger than we imagined it. We thought she was going to collect a few clothes, and she got a store."

One simple idea.

The one factor linking one to thousands.

Designer clothes everywhere.

> *Last week Lindsay and her parents joined Emily Cassidy, another fourteen-year-old, at the opening of a Taylor's Closet in Dallas, Texas. A manufacturer has offered to provide more than 10,000 pieces of clothing. Evidence of the one factor's power to inspire.*

> *The name, Taylor's Closet, is Lindsay's tribute to her twin sister who died at birth. She recognizes that her idea existed in the mind of God long before He placed it in hers. She imagines that Taylor watches from heaven, proud of her for having the courage to follow her dream wherever it leads her.*

HEART GALLERY

A picture is worth a thousand words.
—Barnard

*Sometimes you're just a matchmaker between an idea and the
people destined to implement it. And that's the great thing
about the one factor—you don't have to do it all yourself. You
just have to play your part. Then you sit back and watch.*

Tom stood and watched as several people browsed through his carefully arranged brochures at the back of the church. He struggled to keep
his smile fixed as the frustration and bitterness rose within him. After a
presentation to the congregation describing a foster child's dilemma, less
than a dozen people even bothered to pick up a brochure.

*Don't they care that just a few miles away, children are sitting
in a shelter waiting to be taken to a home?*

Drew felt the same way. As he sat in the back of his church, contem-
plating Tom's words, he knew that his church needed to do something
more than just a three-minute announcement and a table in the lobby.
After a heart-to-heart talk with his pastor, Drew called Tom and asked
him to come back and teach a six-week class on the fatherless.

Tom had never taught a series on the fatherless before, but as the executive director of 4KIDS, he was willing to take advantage of any opportunity to share the reality of the need in his community. He spent hours preparing his topic and made sure he had plenty of handouts.

He drove forty-eight miles to the church.

Twelve people showed up.

It seemed like another wasted effort.

But Matthew was one of the twelve who came to the first class. As Tom spoke, Matthew's passion to be an advocate for the fatherless grew.

One weekend while on a business trip, he saw an in-flight segment on a photographic presentation called the Heart Gallery. This traveling exhibit featured pictures of foster children available for adoption—pictures taken by nationally recognized photographers who brought each child's unique personality to life. As more and more communities mounted their own Heart Gallery exhibits, hundreds of children were adopted around the country. Eight of the adoptions were by photographers engaged in the project.

As Matthew absorbed every picture, his questions grew. Could they do a Heart Gallery in his community? Were there photographers who would be willing to volunteer? What would happen once his co-workers and neighbors were able to see the faces behind the statistics? As a businessman with a background in media, Matthew understood the power of a picture.

Maybe he could make a difference.

When he returned home, Matthew called Drew who, in turn, called Tom. As Matthew started to tell them of his experience, their excitement grew. Tom agreed to contact the community foster care agency while Matthew and Drew used their business experience and contacts to form a non-profit agency and recruit a board of directors. Corporate sponsors lined up, photographers volunteered their time, and the art museum agreed to host the exhibit and promote it at no charge. During the next few months, eighty children were photographed, and more than two hundred local business and community leaders attended the inaugural black-tie gala.

Only God knows how many of the first eighty children will be adopted because of this effort.

But the South Florida Heart Gallery has become a national model. Matthew has recently co-founded the National Heart Gallery, a grass-roots campaign to assist other communities in hosting their own Heart Galleries. One man. One church. One announcement. One class. Tom never saw it coming. Like a single stone tossed into a still pond, his effort caused a ripple effect of Heart Galleries across the country.

Forty-eight miles.

Six weeks.

Twelve people.

It seemed like a monumental waste of time until five of the six couples that attended that class got involved in the Heart Gallery. And that's why this Sunday Tom will be standing in the back of a church somewhere watching people glance at his materials, and as they turn and walk away he'll wonder,

Who's the next Matthew?

ONE INVESTMENT

You are not here to merely make a living.
You are here to enable the world to live more amply with greater vision . . .
You impoverish yourself if you forget this errand.
—Woodrow Wilson

Have you ever wondered where the $20 bill in your pocket has been? Have you ever had that bill before? Will you ever get it again? With millions of bills out there, what are the odds?

Maybe you've wondered about the impact of the money you've spent, invested, or given away. If you could follow it, what would you discover?

Maybe it is framed on a wall somewhere because it was used to pay for the first sale of a new business. One that led to thousands of other sales and then to a series of franchises that led to thousands and thousands of sales.

Or it could have been part of the start-up capital in a company that has revolutionized its industry. Your investment has changed the world and made you a great deal of money in the process.

Or maybe your investment fed a hungry child—a child who will grow up and start an organization to feed and educate poor children around the globe. Your eternal investment has the power to impact thousands of thousands.

The one factor reminds us that an investment doesn't just impact the first place it goes. Its power continues well beyond our sight. This simple truth makes me think twice before I spend or invest my money. One day I will see its full impact.

And that can be very exciting . . . or very sobering.

THE INVESTORS

It is more blessed to give than to receive.[14]
—Jesus

People give in different ways and for different reasons. Over the past decade, 4KIDS has thrived because of the generosity of all sorts of donors, from successful business leaders to struggling single moms. Here are a few of their stories in their own words.

OBEDIENCE: John, College Student

When I first heard there were orphans living in America, I really didn't believe it. But after a little research, I realized I was wrong. Now that I am aware of this problem, I know I am responsible to do something. I don't know everything about the Bible, but I do know that it says, "Faith without works is dead," and that if we know we should do something and don't do it, then it is sin. I also know that feeling bad and saying a quick prayer for those who are in need doesn't relieve me of my responsibility to help. At least that is what I read today in 1 John 3:17 (MSG):

"If you see some brother or sister in need and have the means to do something about it but turn a cold shoulder and do nothing, what happens to God's love? It disappears. And you made it disappear."

I don't want to be the type of person who is fake or insincere. I know God hates that. I want my life as a follower of Jesus to mean something.

I heard a message a few months back that really sealed the deal for me about how to respond to the poor around me. The pastor was talking about how Hebrew farmers were commanded to provide for the orphans and widows by leaving one of their fields unharvested so that the poor could gather wheat.[15] God also required them to give three percent of all their crops to help the needy. We were then challenged to do the same, to give part of our income to help the poor—since it doesn't belong to us anyway.

That is why I give my $40 a month to help the orphans in my neighborhood. I know $40 doesn't solve the problem, or even make a dent for that matter, but I'm not worried about all that. I am focusing on obeying God and doing my part.

After meeting a few of the kids my money has helped, I knew I needed to get even more involved. So now I tell all the people I meet that they can be part of the solution for kids in foster care. Even if they are cash-strapped college kids, they can help those who are close to God's heart. I tell them that this type of obedience will bring them a lot of joy. It did for me.

COMMITMENT: Erin, 4KIDS Staff

As I was writing out the checks for my end-of-the-year giving to a handful of local and international ministries, I was struck by the fact that I had never given to the one I worked for. As an employee, I saw from the inside an organization that worked efficiently to meet a real need in a very tangible way. Sure I had encouraged others to give, but why hadn't I? At first it seemed a little strange to write a check back to the organization that wrote me checks twice a month, but the more I thought about it, the more I was convinced.

Now every two weeks I give an offering out of my own paycheck back to the ministry. I do this because this is not just a job to me—it is my life's work, and I know that wherever my treasure is, there my heart will be also.

This principle has changed the way I look at my job. I now see it as employee ownership. It's not about how I would spend other people's money but rather how I would spend mine. Now I turn the lights off when I leave my office. I try to find something used before I buy it new. I work harder to find volunteers. My heart has followed my investment.

I'm amazed to see how much this simple truth has changed my perspective.

SACRIFICE: Kristen, Single Mom

I've wanted to give money to help those in need for a long time, but I could never find that extra $20 at the end of the month. As a single mom, things are so tight. I knew God wanted me to make a sacrifice, but I still wrestled with it. I wanted a newer car, but I also wanted to help those less fortunate than I. I couldn't do both. I made the right decision. I still drive my old car, but I feel whole.

That's better than driving a new car.

At first, I would write the check every month and say a quick prayer for the kids it was helping, but then I got curious. That's when I went to see where my sacrifice was making a difference. I went on a tour of the foster homes and realized it was time for another sacrifice. I needed to give something even scarcer than my money. I was supposed to give my time. So now I volunteer at the shelter one Saturday a month for a few hours.

I know God sees these sacrifices and is pleased with them, but the most surprising thing about sacrificing is the benefit you get back. Even with the sacrifice, I still have money, and I still have free time. I just enjoy them more than I did before.

COMMUNITY IMPACT: Mark, Pastor

Every pastor wants to impact the community around him. When we looked at the community where our church is, we saw the huge need that existed for children in foster care. There were not enough good homes for kids in crisis to go to. It was clearly the biggest need in our community, one for which nobody seemed to have a good answer.

Our leadership team began to ask what would happen if a church focused its resources and people on this one big issue. Could we take it down?

What started as a crazy idea led to a series of thoughtful discussions and then to action. Instead of scattering our resources on a hundred community issues with little visible impact, we decided to take a large step of faith and commit a significant amount of support and staff to minister to this need. It certainly had God's heart, and now it had our heart as well. We believed we could radically change foster care and lead other churches to do the same. If we were successful, we knew people would see the church as that city on a hill, a beacon of power and love, bringing hope to those who had none.

Ten years later we look back, and the seed we planted has grown into a huge tree. Our financial investment has paid off, maybe not monetarily, but in changed lives and in our community's recognition that the church has significance—and that God and His people still have the will and the heart to reach out to those most vulnerable. Most of all, we learned that if the church follows its mandate to care for orphans and widows, God will bless it in a way that is beyond anything we could think or imagine.

YIELD: Scott, CEO

As an investor, yield is very important to me. I am always assessing opportunities, evaluating risks, and predicting potential returns on my investments.

Jesus told a story that epitomizes my mode of thinking. It was about a farmer who scattered his seeds in a field. It seems from the story that most of his seeds (75%) were wasted. Some of his seeds, however, had a 300, 600, or 1,000% return. In the investment world I live in, a 30–50% return is excellent. The return Jesus describes is mind-boggling.[16]

A few years ago these thoughts dominated my mind. I was looking for an investment into God's work on Earth. I found 4KIDS and invested some money. As I look back at the yield, I see hundreds of kids who have been restored to their families and who have also experienced a heart and life change.

I think this is the best investment I've ever made . . . because it is generational. Not only are the lives of these kids better, but they will one day have the chance to show this kind of love to their kids. Even more, the investment is eternal because many of these children and their families have come to embrace Jesus as their Savior.

I believe heaven will be different because I took this risk and put my money where my heart is. I can't wait to be approached in heaven and feel the tug on my sleeve and finally have the chance to see their faces. I think that will be a pretty good day.

GRATITUDE: Gabrielle, Former Foster Child

I am rich.

I have less than $300 in the bank, but I know I'm rich. I grew up on and off the streets, dropping in and out of school. A lot of nights I had no food. And then one day, I had no family. I was abandoned.

Now things couldn't be more different. I just graduated from high school, and I start college next week. I have a job. My fridge and closet are full. Most importantly, I have a family, and I know God.

I am rich.

Being rich isn't about money. It's really about perspective. I am rich because I see how much God has filled my life. When I was desperate, He not only provided me food, clothes, and shelter, but also gave me hope.

Now it's my turn to give back. After everything God has done for me, there shouldn't be anything I wouldn't give back to Him. I give money to help other kids like me. It's a gratitude thing! I know five years ago someone gave, and that money helped save me. I know where the money goes, and I feel a strong sense of satisfaction in knowing that I am helping another young person get the opportunity I got. And that makes me even more grateful!

INSPIRATION: Festus and Helen Stacy Foundation

We knew our community had a problem. Kids shouldn't be abused by the system that's supposed to protect them. Kids shouldn't sleep in office buildings. We wanted to help but needed direction. One Sunday our pastor shared a vision to solve this crisis. We met with him and a few key leaders and realized God had given many of them the same understanding of the problem and the same desire to fix it. We knew we were being led to make a significant financial investment in this God-sized project, to make this vision a reality. So we stepped up to the plate.

In the past we were what you might call "pew potatoes." We came to church, lived a good life, and went home, but it was our investment in eternal things that finally got us out of the pew and onto the playing field.

Looking back, we realize that the only things of true and lasting value here on planet Earth are our investments into the eternal. We see this through a home like KidsPlace, one of our first investments in foster care. Two hundred children came through this home in the first five years. All of them had the chance to experience the love of Jesus during a time of crisis.

Anytime we visit, the smiles of the kids remind us why we invested in foster care. This is our community. These are our children. They have been through so much, but you can see hope alive in their eyes. Knowing we were a catalyst for this gives us an indescribable feeling inside. It is a sense of accomplishment, deep satisfaction, and great joy. No feeling can compare. We should have bought ten of them.

Ultimately, we know it was God's money, not ours. His vision, not our pastor's. His compassion, not ours. But He used us and changed us in the process to be a little more like Him. For that, the glory is His and His alone!

All these reasons for giving make me look back at my checking account and want to do things a bit differently. After all, we can't take it with us, and when we die other people will decide how to spend it. But we have the power right now. And that power affects eternity itself.

Have you made any eternal investments lately?

ONE PASSION

When you set yourself on fire,
people love to come and see you burn.
—John Wesley

As I was writing this chapter, I began to think about my closest friends. All six are foster or adoptive parents. How did this happen? Did we become friends because they had a heart for kids? Or did they take in kids because we were friends? Which came first?

Looking back, only one of my friends was an adoptive parent before I met him. For the rest of us, it just kind of happened. None of us ever said to the other, "You should do this."

But passion is contagious. It's like the flu. You catch it when the people around you are infected.

This is the invigorating nature of the one factor. We all had a common passion to help disadvantaged children, and then one of us took in a child. We all looked on, and it began—more and more—to seem like the obvious thing to do. One by one, we made the choice to invite children into our families. When it came down to the last of our group, the passion had spread so thoroughly, there really was no choice. It was almost irresistible.

Now it all seems so normal that we don't think twice about it. When we all get together, we can see the curious stares. With all the colors in our families, it's hard to figure out who belongs to whom. But as a group of friends, we know we have been caught up in something amazing.

I hope you have friends like this—friends who don't just complain that there are too many problems in the world but who do something about it. And together you become a mini-movement (all movements are at first mini).

If you wish this were true, but it isn't yet, maybe you will be the first one to find this passion and infect others with it, spreading it to your circle of friends. Sometimes it is stories like Tyrone's that can ignite that passion.

WHILE THE CHURCH WAS SLEEPING

. . . it is high time to awake out of sleep . . . [17]
—Paul, the Apostle

*In our politically-charged world, we fight over so many issues.
We argue about definitions and fight for "rights." Sometimes in
a passionate belief to be against something, we miss what or
whom we're really "for" and end up missing the whole point.*

Tyrone needed a home. The whirlwind that brought him to SafePlace
was a tragically familiar story—no dad, and a mother trying to raise three
children all by herself. The pressure led her to escape from life into crys-
tal meth. Tyrone's younger brother and sister found a foster home within
twenty-four hours of being removed from their mother, but there was no
home offered to Tyrone.

The problem? Tyrone was a sixteen-year-old African American. Although friendly, respectful, and a straight-A student, he was fighting a
stigma he couldn't see. After several days of waiting, he realized it might
be a long time before a family could be found to take him.

To pass the time, Tyrone spent his days talking to Jym, a staff supervi-
sor of SafePlace. He talked about his life, his dreams, and some of the fears

he had for his younger brother and sister. Jym began to enjoy their talks. Seldom had he seen such thoughtful insight from a teenager. They talked about God and His plans for Tyrone's life. Tyrone asked Jym about his experiences in life and the trials that had brought him to faith in God. Tyrone asked Jym to pray that God would find him a home. Jym prayed with Tyrone but couldn't keep from wondering, *Where is the Church?*

The following day the placement unit called with good news. A home had been found for Tyrone. The couple arrived a few hours later, but they were not what Tyrone had expected. Two men greeted him at the door. He exchanged glances with Jym, who returned the surprised look. Tyrone shifted awkwardly as he looked down at his feet. He was clearly very uncomfortable with the idea of living with a homosexual couple.

Tyrone asked to speak to Jym privately, so they retreated to a quiet corner. Tyrone wondered aloud what the odds were that another family would come forward to take him. He had already been sleeping in an office building for three days. Jym said that he didn't know for sure. They both stood as if frozen in time while Tyrone contemplated his decision. Then, reluctantly, Tyrone gathered his things, stuffed them in his backpack, and headed for the front door.

For the next few months, or possibly years, this would be his home. As he walked out the front door, he glanced back at Jym one last time. Jym was overcome by a complete sense of helplessness, and that's when he uttered a prayer with great potential:

"God, please wake up your Church for the next Tyrone."

UNDERCOVER HEROES

I am only one; but still I am one.
I cannot do everything, but I can do something;
I will not refuse to do something I can do.
—Helen Keller

I was thinking about my heroes the other day and how they've changed over my lifetime. First there were Superman and Flash. (I always wondered who would win if they ever fought.) Then I progressed to real-life fire fighters. After that, my heroes were my favorite athletes. They all seemed to have the ability to excel at the perfect moment in time; they embodied all I wanted to be. I guess this is why we say our heroes are larger than life.

But my heroes are different these days. They mostly go unnoticed in real life. I see them up all night rocking a crack-addicted newborn. I see them on the phone for hours with school counselors working to find a breakthrough that may never come. They give up their time, money, and privacy to serve an often-thankless group.

These heroes of mine may go unnoticed now, but in eternity things will be much different. Fifteen minutes of fame won't exist on the other side. Their Audience of One will be all that matters. Let me introduce you to a few of my heroes.

ANDRE: Housedad, GuysPlace

I've always loved kids. I came from a large family, and I was always in the caretaker role. I guess that's what the pastor in my church noticed in me when he suggested I mentor a boy in the church who had no dad in his life. I took on the challenge and loved it.

A year or so later, the same pastor asked if I had ever considered working with foster children. Always open to the next challenge, I became a foster parent and took in a young man no one else was willing to take. A few weeks later, another phone call, another teenage boy. Several months later my pastor asked me to become a full-time houseparent. By then I had five teenage boys living with me.

They warned me that this experience was a little like drinking out of a fire hose. (There is no easy way to do it, and you'll never be the same again). Now I know why they chuckled when they said it. They were right. This has been the most difficult and rewarding thing I have ever done. The highs are really high, and the lows really low. Over the last five years, I've learned things about myself I never would've learned otherwise, like the fact that I need more help than I'd like to admit. A single guy raising five boys requires a person to ask for help. My mom, grandmom, brothers, and sisters are over all the time. They have all become family to my boys.

After a few years and raising more than a dozen boys, God brought a woman into my life. I told her I came as a package of six, and she married me anyway. These days the house is a bit cleaner, and the love is stronger than ever. I don't know how to retire from this. We may end up taking all the boys with us when we retire from house parenting.

How do you say goodbye to family?

DIANA: Foster Parent

I always wanted a girl, but my husband and I were unable to have one. Our first few foster children were boys, and then came Mimi. She was the most beautiful little girl I had ever seen. She was only a few weeks old when she came into our house, and my heart was gone the moment I set eyes on her. They told us in foster parent training not to get too attached, but after the first few weeks, it was definitely too late.

Mimi's biological mother was 21, and her three other children were removed from her home because of drug use. As hard as it was, my husband and I prayed for her to get her life back together. We invited her to our church and over to our house for Mimi's birthday. We knew Mimi's future was not in our control, but we were not adequately prepared for the phone call. After a year and a half, Mimi was going back to live with her biological mother. She was thriving with us, but she was not ours.

I really struggled with this. In my head I knew it was something I had to let go of—but selfishly I wanted to keep Mimi because I knew we could provide her with a more stable home. How could a 23-year-old mom who was just getting over a drug problem take care of four children? Mimi's mother had unstable housing and sporadic employment, and she was surrounded by poor role models. All this added to my own heartache. I felt like I was giving away my child to an unfit parent.

God knew I needed help to process this situation so I could have a better perspective. I found that perspective while reading the Bible one morning. It was a story about a woman named Hannah.[18] Like me, she couldn't have children so she made a promise to God that if she had a son, she would dedicate him to the Lord. God answered and gave her the child she wanted so badly, but then she had to keep her vow and take him to live in the temple. I wondered if she second-guessed her vow.

I know Hannah must have been so torn up inside when she dropped off her son, Samuel, to Eli, the priest. Hannah was definitely the better parent and had the more stable home. (Eli was an obese 90-year-old single dad with two out-of-control sons of his own). But Hannah knew that Samuel did not belong to her. He belonged to God and, because of that, she was not going to attempt to manipulate something she shouldn't.

Hannah gave Samuel back to the God who had given him to her, and God protected Samuel through the process. Samuel thrived and grew into a great leader, in spite of his dysfunctional family. I had to get to the place where I knew that God was doing the same for Mimi.

That was three years ago, and now I see a little more of God's plan. He re-united Mimi, her mom, and her grandmother; an entire family has been restored. Now when I think of Mimi, the pain has been replaced with peace. I now see that my own narrow, selfish perspective is not always the best view. God has a better view, and He knows what He's doing.

PATTY: Single Parent

As a single mom raising a teenage son, life can be tough. I guess that is why I was so close to my church; they always seemed to guide me in the right direction with my son. They helped me with my parenting skills and provided a mentor for my son.

Then it struck me one day that I should give back. So I volunteered to babysit foster children. As I watched their lives, I felt a growing desire to do more, but I was a single mom struggling myself. How could I possibly help? I took the foster parent training class anyway. I had to do something.

After a home study and a mountain of paperwork, we got our first child, a five-year-old boy. My son and I took on this new challenge, and we actually worked together as a team. Then I got a promotion at work and realized I could buy a new house with a few more bedrooms. Before long I had three foster children plus my son.

There were many days where the sacrifice seemed too great, and I wanted to give up. But when one of my foster children almost died, God provided me with a rare moment of clarity: this is what I am supposed to do, and nothing else matters. Some people are out there waiting to be "called by God" to do this.

To me it's simple: the need is the call.

People thought I was crazy—a single mom with four kids. People asked, "How can you take in kids and then give them back?" I wanted to respond, "Would you rather they sleep on a bus bench?"

I have realized that not everyone will understand. I've even lost a few friends through this, but I've discovered that there are also people who will be there, day and night, to help me out.

I guess this journey for me has been about my own redemption. You see, when I was in my twenties I permanently lost custody of my first son because of drugs and alcohol. I had been declared an unfit parent. This wound kept me up many nights as I thought about that failure and loss. God not only set me free from these addictions, but He put me back in the very place where I had failed, and said, "Try this again."

Foster care has given me a tremendous gift. It made me aware of how conditional my love had been. I only loved people who loved me. Now I think I love a little more like God does, and that feeling is like no other.

ALMOST A HERO

Love anything and your heart will be wrung and possibly broken.
If you want to make sure of keeping it intact you must give it to no one . . .
Wrap it carefully round with hobbies and little luxuries; avoid all
entanglements. Lock it up safe in the casket or coffin of your selfishness.
But in that casket—safe, dark, motionless, airless—it will change.
It will not be broken; it will become unbreakable, impenetrable,
irredeemable. To love is to be vulnerable.
—C.S. Lewis

Passion doesn't always have a happily-ever-after ending. Sometimes passion leads you down a path that looks like it will make you a hero and then, without warning, the road detours. Now you're sitting there in your failure wondering why you went on this trip in the first place. But failure is a great teacher, and if you can sort through your expectations, you may find a more deeply held belief that will lead to an even greater success. My wife, Suzanne, and I learned this best through our first foster care experience.

Suzanne and I have always had a heart for disadvantaged children. Within the first year of marriage, we went to a foster parent training orientation to see if this was something we should pursue. They told us that it usually takes people two or three years from the time they first hear about the need to the time they actually take a child into their home. I guess we are slow learners because it took us six years. After the orientation we had great intentions, but life just got busy.

During the next few years, we kept hearing about the need and really felt compelled to do something, but it just never seemed to be the right time. That was until we met Sean during my first year working at 4KIDS. At first glance, he was just another normal fifteen-year-old. We would play basketball together and every once in a while he came over for dinner. Later we found out he had been in twenty-eight different foster homes in three years.

Then one day his foster home placement fell apart, and he couldn't live there any more. I remember praying that week, "God, find Sean a home." I knew in the back of my mind that if there were no homes available, our family might very well be the answer to that prayer. All the reasons we shouldn't were right in front of us again. We had our two-year-old adopted son, Jackson, and Suzanne was nine months pregnant with our son, Kaden.

I'll never forget the night my wife and I first talked about taking Sean into our home. We were at a restaurant on a date, and I didn't know how to tell her what was happening in my heart. So I just threw it out there between the salad and main course: "What do you think about taking Sean into our house?"

Her reply shocked me: "I think we should take him in." I sat there kind of stunned. This was an open-ended commitment, and it could very well be for a lifetime. But God had been stirring her heart at the same time He was guiding mine.

After three weeks of searching, there was only one home available.

Ours.

We were really naive when we signed up to be foster parents. We thought we were going to be heroes; our love for Sean (or any child for that matter) would ensure success. We had agreed to treat Sean as if he were our own son. He was big brother to our sons Jackson and Kaden. We spent hours in the evenings getting him caught up in school and worked even harder trying to create a more positive peer group for him. He learned what a family was, and even called us mom and dad. It was everything we had hoped it would be . . . and more.

He wrote us a letter one year later and asked us to adopt him. That was one of the best days of my life. But then just a few weeks later, he ran away to find his biological parents. Stunned would be an understatement.

He dropped out of school and in a few weeks spent all the money he had saved during the year. There was an attraction we could not compete against. After the shock wore off, we were left with the sick feeling that all the love, all the hours, all the prayers we invested were in vain. For the first few weeks I was a complete basket case. I constantly checked the caller ID and looked out the window, thinking he would come home. But he didn't. I had never been hurt that badly before, not ever. I could feel cynicism growing inside of me. I will definitely never do this again. What's the point? This question consumed my thoughts for weeks.

Then one night I was reading the story of King David and his mighty men.[19] Before David was king of Israel, he was the general of a militia army on the run from a jealous king who wanted him dead. After years of being away from home, he wished out loud for a drink of water from the well in Jerusalem. Three of his bravest warriors heard his wish and snuck behind enemy lines to get him a drink of water from that well. When they brought David the water, he couldn't believe they had actually risked their lives to give him this gift. He refused to accept it because he considered it too valuable. So David gave the gift to the only person worthy of such a sacrifice—God.

He poured it out onto the ground, as if to say, *God, this is for you.*

Do you ever have moments like that? Moments where you just get it? For me, reading David's story was one of those moments. Our service to

Sean was not a waste. Even if there were no visible effects, except for our broken hearts, the year we poured our lives into Sean was an extravagant gift to our King. If things had worked out as we expected, we would have been heroes. It would have been more about us than about God, about how hard we worked to turn it all around. With the reality of failure staring us in the face, we were forced to conclude that the last year of our lives was either a colossal waste or the greatest sign of love for God that we could possibly show—a gift few would recognize. Even some family members and friends looked at our efforts as a waste.

We've had other foster children, and we eventually adopted our youngest son, Kennedy, from foster care. We have experienced the "success" we initially anticipated. We followed a passion that is still molding our family to this day. Although sometimes my wife and I would like to trade that first year if we had the chance, ultimately, we wouldn't. That year was our offering to God. One He is worthy of.

TAKING YOUR WORK HOME

Leaders are visionaries with a poorly developed sense of fear
and no concept of the odds against them.
—Robert Jarvik

"Taking your work home" conjures up images of misplaced priorities and a lack of balance between your occupation and your family. If you're a leader, sometimes you get caught up in the vision and realize you are in way over your head. At that point you have to stop, evaluate your priorities, and ask if the venture is worth the sacrifice. Each of the leaders I work with at 4KIDS has gone on that soul search and answered yes—because the work they take home is more important than most. Their work is helping children who are hurting. Nine to five cannot contain that passion.

The men and women who lead our team could easily make more money elsewhere. They could work fewer hours with less emotional involvement. They could experience less harrowing work assignments and less stress, but for some reason they choose to stay. Most of them describe their passion to help kids as something beyond an ordinary job assignment. They talk as if they are on a mission, as if their efforts could somehow change the world. They speak from first-hand experience since many of them live with the results of their work.

Joan has taken home her share of kids. As a trainer for foster parents, she prepares ordinary couples and singles for the work she has been doing for years. Her home has welcomed many teenagers, who to this day still call her mom. For some, it is the only stable home they have ever known. Joan is able to speak to new foster parents with a conviction born of her own experiences.

Ken, director of the Independent Living Program, can be found every Thursday night eating dinner with a group of young men struggling to define what family looks like. A school teacher and houseparent before he came to 4KIDS, Ken and his wife, Liz (already parents to four children) adopted one of their foster children, Julia. The only reason they stopped taking foster children last year was because there was no more room left in their house.

Erin, director of the Residential Program, has always had a room or two available in her apartment for stray girls who needed a home. First it was the girl fighting to kick a drug habit. Then it was a young woman experiencing a crisis pregnancy and needing a place to get back on her feet. After that it was a girl battling inner demons and thoughts of suicide. Through the late nights, countless trips to the hospital, tears, and prayers, Erin has been a big sister to many of the girls who have crossed her path. For Erin, there is no delineation between work and private life. It is all lived out together. Erin was married a few months back and her passion has infected her husband. They are in the process of adopting two teenage girls.

Mat, director of Programs, and his wife, Spring, worked in the social service field for almost ten years. He served as a director of residential programs; she, as a classroom aide for children with autism. They decided to take home children no one else wanted to help—medically fragile children. To be able to take them from the shelter that had been their only home, Mat and Spring were trained like medical professionals as they learned to care for their immune-compromised sons. They have adopted two boys, Jay and Charlie, and are in the process of adopting a girl, Emily.

Tom is the executive director. Tom worked as a housedad in a group home for three years with his wife, Linda. When he speaks of that time, tears fill his eyes. Every one of his tears seems to strengthen his resolve to change just one more life. It is not uncommon for Tom and Linda, in their empty-nest stage of life, to be seen tromping through a park with toddlers as they provide a much-needed break for other foster parents.

Countless staff members and volunteers have joined our team only to find themselves unwilling to restrict their involvement to just a few hours a week. This infectious spirit has even extended to members of the board of directors. Matt owns an area law firm and David a successful construction company. Neither could avoid keeping their involvement limited to a quarterly meeting. Both men and their families have taken the leap from advocate to full-time foster parents.

When you speak with any member of our leadership team, you won't get an ivory-tower story. There are no rose-colored glasses. No pipe dreams. Instead, you'll hear about what it feels like to be in over your head, working on the clock and off, facing exhaustion, enduring pain, sweating, and shedding tears on the way to seeing a single life changed. The faces that greet them at the door at the end of the day are the tangible products of their work—their own foster and adopted children, redeemed.

That's what fuels the passion. That's why tears still flow freely when we see the devastation in children's lives caused by the sins of others. It reminds us why we first took our children home. And it reminds us how far they have come.

If only we could find one more person willing to cross the line of professional balance and boundaries, someone crazy enough to jump head-first into the redemption experience by taking his or her work home.

ONE SOURCE

How could one man chase a thousand . . .
unless the LORD had given them up? [20]
—Moses

There's a book that tells of the Song of Moses. You know, the man who led the Hebrew people out of Egypt after four hundred years of slavery. In the song, there's a line that makes me think about the one factor: "How could one man chase a thousand?"[21]

Think about it with me.

One chases a thousand.

How does that happen?

A small outmanned, overmatched group fights against overwhelming odds and wins. Do we chalk it up as dumb luck or just good fortune? Is this the product of random chance, where every so often someone hits the jackpot?

A few years after Moses, Israel has another hero. A rock from his sling finds its way into a giant's forehead, making a young boy a hero for all time. Was it a lucky shot, or did something guide the trajectory of that stone? That one stone changed the history of the world. It set off a chain reaction of events that put the nation of Israel on the map forever. The one factor phenomenon is neither random nor coincidence. It derives its power from God.

It is Divinity undercover.[22]

When God intervenes in time, He often uses us to do what He could do all on His own, lining up people and moments to seismically shift the events of history. People like Abraham Lincoln and Martin Luther King Jr. become the epicenter.

God knows the world needs changing, and He enjoys using people like you and me to do it. All of our greatest ideas and passions were His first. His influence starts the ball rolling and allows the momentum to impact the world. The Bible illustrates over and over again that God prefers to use things that seem insignificant to achieve His ultimate plan.

He makes the small, big. A baby named Moses in a basket. Deliverance of an entire nation.

He makes the big, small. The redemption of the world. One Son.

When I look back at the last ten years and review these stories, I see something bigger than all of us at work. He created one woman, who knocked on doors until one opened. He prompted one man, a firefighter, who become father of the year. He put the idea of a clothing store for foster kids into the mind of one teenage girl. He allowed one organization to create signs with His name to generate income that is still helping children at KidsPlace.

Today someone a lot like you will make a decision that will change everything. And there will be no trumpets.

No applause.

No real sign that the decision made any difference at all. But the God of the one factor will use that decision to change a destiny, a destiny that may change a thousand more.

That's why Moses wrote that song. It encapsulated his life. One idea helped him escape genocide in a basket. One person took him from the river and adopted him. One moment made him a fugitive. ONE called him from obscurity to an impossible mission. ONE used him, a stutterer, to speak for an entire nation. One passion drove him to deliver his people.

The Source of the one factor, weaving people and circumstances, allowed one man to chase a thousand. And at the end of Moses' life you can hear his conviction grow. His question becomes a statement. His song has become his experience.

Five of you will chase a hundred, and a hundred of you will chase ten thousand . . . [23]

But Moses' influence did not end there. Even after his death, the people of Israel continued to sing his song. Generations later, that song caught up with a young shepherd with five stones and a slingshot. On the day David met the giant, it may have been Moses' song he hummed in his head as he charged . . . and chased a thousand himself.

Hundreds of years after his death, God used Moses' experience and his song to create a ripple effect that will never fully be traced out. Thousands of years after his death, one of those ripples could be you.

We know there are still giants.

We know the world needs changing.

Moses' experience is our opportunity. God has given us the privilege of participating in His redemption of the planet, and this is the greatest adventure of all. Remaking the world. This is what we are invited to do.[24]

Maybe the objections are already lining up in your head. Maybe you can't see how God could use someone like you. But before you close the door on the opportunity, think about where Moses came from: refugee, murderer, fugitive.

Remember, Moses was forgotten in the desert for forty years, but God was not done with him.

And He is not done with you.

HELL'S NIGHTMARE

Fairy tales do not tell children that dragons exist.
Children already know that dragons exist.
Fairy tales tell children the dragons can be killed.
—G. K. Chesterton

When I was 18 (back when I knew everything), I struggled with the whole idea of good and evil in this sort of cosmic battle. It seemed so much like a story someone made up to explain why people did heroic or stupid things. But as I've watched life happen, I am more convinced than ever that there are very real powers at work. Unseen, but very real. These powers are revealed in the best and worst of what we see in the world and in what we see in our dreams and in our nightmares.

Nightmares can be terrifying. I'm always glad when I wake up and realize that I have my life back. But what if you couldn't wake up from your nightmare? What if you opened your eyes and the terror remained?

Domestic violence, drug use, sexual abuse, abandonment. These atrocities occur in the shadows, in the secret places, threatening the most precious commodity a child possesses: hope.

Like handprints in wet cement, abuse leaves a permanent mark on the behavior and thoughts of its young victims. When drugs devastate a family, children learn early on that their relative value is not as great as their parents' drug of choice. Sexual abuse strips away the innocence of childhood, and without skilled intervention, the violation and betrayal will only reproduce itself, sabotaging future relationships. Abandonment and the resulting identity crisis remind children that they are not worth staying for.

We must recognize that there is a very real enemy at work. His strategy is simple. Steal. Kill. Destroy. [25]

GOD'S DREAM

. . . no mind has conceived what God has prepared
for those who love him.[26]
—The apostle Paul, quoting the prophet Isaiah

For abused and abandoned children, when life is the nightmare, dreams can serve as an escape. Imagination provides a brief intermission from the reality of a life filled with pain, rejection, and loneliness. For the modern-day orphan, a happy childhood may be beyond their grasp . . . but not beyond their imagination.

What do these children of sorrow dream about? Some dream of a house, a family, and a full stomach. Some dream of a birthday party where, for just a moment in time, they are the center of attention. These dreams shout, "You matter to us." But will these dreams ever become reality?

Across town, another group dreams. This group dreams of making a difference in the world. They dream of leaving their legacies by helping the lost boys and girls of this world. They dream of being a Big Brother or Big Sister to a child who has never had one. They dream of filling their empty bedrooms with the stories, clutter, and the contagious laughter of children—children who will hug and kiss them and call them mom and dad, transforming them both in the process.

Where do these dreams come from?

They come from the Dream Giver, God Almighty. He uses these dreams to give us a glimpse into His divine imagination. In God's dream, the lonely, rejected, and abandoned children of this world are restored. They feast at great tables and cry no more tears. They find a place of perfect protection, uninterrupted acceptance, and unspeakable joy. It is a place where those who extend themselves to serve the needy find great reward.

This has been our Father's dream since before the beginning of time. It is the place where all things become new. It is a place called heaven. But this God of dreams is not satisfied to wait until heaven. Throughout the pages of His Book, we see He has made provision for the present reality.

God calls himself a Father to the fatherless. Until heaven, His provision for the fatherless is amazingly simple. It is nothing mystical, nothing mysterious. "God sets the lonely in families." [27] A family is God's answer to a lonely child's prayer.

Every day God is making dreams come alive and nightmares fade as He matches those searching for lasting purpose with those who need love and acceptance. Tomorrow, another orphan will pray the Lord's Prayer, ". . . your kingdom come, your will be done on earth as it is in heaven . . ." and God will make this desperate plea a reality. [28]

God is inviting you into His dream.

ANSWERING JESUS' PRAYER

I pray also for those who will believe in me through their message,
that all of them may be one . . . [29]
—Jesus

In the final hours of life, this was a dying man's plea. Jesus prayed that His followers would be one—a 2,000-year-old prayer that still waits unanswered. Did Jesus make an impossible request?

At the core of all of us, we know that nothing is impossible for God. But practically, you have to wonder how this unity can happen.

As we scroll through history, we've seen glimpses of this unity. In a common fight against social and political injustice, the church has often joined forces across denominational and racial barriers and proven it is a force to be reckoned with. The abolition of slavery, the fall of communism, and the Civil Rights Movement saw Catholics, Baptists, Presbyterians, Pentecostals, and Orthodox believers all lay down their differences and carry a common banner—and for the briefest of moments the world witnessed the power of Jesus' prayer. Is there a cause that compelling today? One the church could not ignore?

In December 2002 a handful of Christian leaders met in the cramped upstairs office of an inner-city church to brainstorm. It was an unlikely cross-section of urban and mega churches, African-American and white churches, denominational and para-church ministries. They agreed to ask a few vital questions:

What is the biggest problem in our community?

How could this problem be a tool to forge partnerships and see real unity?

After thoughtful discussion they crafted a plan. There was no greater problem in their community than orphaned children. No more compelling and less polarizing issue than their care. After all, caring for the fatherless was not simply one of many good ideas; it was a biblical mandate. It is the very definition of pure religion. They prayed that day for God to make the meeting into a movement.

Some things were clear. The task before them was enormous. The institutional obstacles of church-state friction, denominational isolation, and racial segregation were daunting, but it was also clear that this task could only be accomplished together. They would need to begin acting as one agency, one Church, and one body.

That December, Churches United for Foster Care was born. The strategy was simple: raise awareness of the problem and provide necessary support for the churches that joined the effort. As a group, they committed to sharing information and resources. They would evaluate their progress after one year.

That first year was a year of building relationships, regular meetings, and serious prayer. Barriers started falling. Unity was in motion. One year later, we celebrated the results at a community breakfast:

782 children provided shelter

70 church partners

57 foster homes

17 adoptions

Churches were connecting around the most vital community issue, and the ripple effect was felt throughout South Florida. The following year witnessed more church presentations and a growing advocacy among existing partners. Two years into the vision, we celebrated even more lives changed:

995 children provided shelter

25 new church partners

76 new foster homes

34 more adoptions

Momentum was growing. The social service community began to take notice. A viable solution to a community problem was being substantially met by churches. Three years into the vision, more than four hundred people gathered to celebrate:

1,234 children provided shelter

35 new church partners

119 new foster homes

35 more adoptions

Four years into the vision, the progress continued to amaze us. Something bigger than our effort was at work.

1,346 children provided shelter

40 new church partners

185 new foster homes

71 more adoptions

In four short years, the totals were beyond what any of us had expected:

4,357 children provided shelter

170 church partners

437 total foster homes

157 adoptions

The unity experiment had been successful, the upstairs prayer answered. The meeting was now a movement.

Psalm 133 speaks about the power unleashed in unity. When God sees it, He commands a blessing.[30] I don't know if any of the men and women in that upstairs office realized the power they were unlocking by the simple desire to achieve unity, but when a Father wants to answer His Son's dying wish, there are few things He will allow to stand in His way.

YOUR INHERITANCE

The legacy we leave is not just in our possessions,
but in the quality of our lives. What preparations should we be making now?
The greatest waste in all of our earth, which cannot be recycled or reclaimed,
is our waste of the time that God has given us each day.
—Billy Graham

It's a phone call you may have dreamt about. A voice on the other end informs you that a distant relative has passed away and left you his fortune. In an instant, your life is changed. Your inheritance has found you, and you will never be the same.

What would you think of someone who refused to take the steps necessary to claim this windfall? I mean the paperwork was too overwhelming—so many phone calls, lawyers, flights, hassles. Just forget the whole thing. We would all call that person crazy. You don't calculate work or obligation in the light of such a payoff. The tasks are not chores to avoid but steps to access the opportunity of a lifetime.

God has left us an inheritance. And it's right in front of you. Most of us walk by it every day, probably because we don't recognize it. This inheritance is far better than a financial jackpot, but it comes disguised so only the most curious seeker enjoys it.

Interested?

God's inheritance to us is the weak, poor, and lost of this world. Not exactly what you expected, but take a minute to unpack this truth. If we really believe God loves us and has the best in mind for us, then maybe this concept warrants a second look. Over and over in the Bible we see God command His people to defend the fatherless, the widow, and the stranger.

. . . learn to do right! Seek justice, encourage the oppressed. Defend the cause of the fatherless, plead the case of the widow. —Isaiah 1:17 (NIV)

. . . the aliens, the fatherless and the widows who live in your towns may come and eat and be satisfied, and so that the LORD your God may bless you in all the work of your hands. —Deuteronomy 14:29 (NIV)

God's instructions regarding the poor and weak do not only come in the form of commands, but they are also presented as opportunities.

If you help the poor, you are lending to the Lord—and he will repay you! —Proverbs 19:17 (NLT)

The kingdom of heaven is like treasure hidden in a field. When a man found it, he hid it again, and then in his joy went and sold all he had and bought that field. —Matthew 13:44 (NIV)

Loaning God money.

Buried treasure.

If these ideas sound intriguing, it is by design. They are intended to lead us down a path. God is not trying to trick us. He doesn't need our time or money. At the end of the path is treasure. The discovery is for us. Let me prove it to you.

Who are the happiest, most content people you know? They are probably the most generous people you know. Most likely, they are the ones who consistently serve others, with little thought to themselves, and have a great time doing it. They have found a liberty in service to the less fortunate and a joy that those who have walked past this buried treasure rarely know.

Have you discovered this treasure? If you haven't yet, here are three things I have learned along the way:

When you take care of the poor and the weak, you will begin to see yourself in them. I don't naturally see myself as needy and vulnerable. I have a wife and a family, and I live in a nice house. With a college education, a good job, and money in the bank, I am fairly independent and self-sufficient. But as I interact with kids who have such clear needs, God seems to whisper in my ear,

> *That's you, Doug. You are that weak and vulnerable. When I found you, you were like an abandoned child that no one wanted, but I claimed you.[31] You are not as self-made as you think.*

And that whisper is a gift.

It reminds me of who I am and how much I need help in my own life.

When you work with the marginalized and forgotten, you begin to catch glimpses of Jesus. The Bible describes the coming judgment where people are sorted by how they cared for the poor, the naked, the sick, and the destitute.[32] The people who cared for the hungry, naked, and lonely go to the right and receive an amazing inheritance. Those who didn't help this often-forgotten group go to the left and are judged because they didn't recognize Jesus in His disguise.

Everyone is surprised to find out that Jesus was undercover. None of them would've walked by Jesus begging on the street. Not many of us would leave Jesus at SafePlace, without a home, unless we didn't recognize Him. Today Jesus has His disguise on, appearing as those who take from us and appear to have nothing to give. If you decide to get into the game, hide and seek can be a lot of fun.

When you care for the fatherless, you share God's joy. When you see an adopted child thriving in a family, your initial thoughts may be that the child is fortunate. I used to think that, until I adopted Jackson and Kennedy. Now I know I am the blessed one. I am sharing the joy of God. The Bible reveals that it was God's will and pleasure to adopt us into His family.[33] God adopted us because He wanted to. As we choose to become parents to the fatherless, we get a rare glimpse into the joy God feels. Heaven rejoices every time someone discovers their Father. The reward is a joy so profound and lasting that words fail to describe it.

So what about the inheritance God has left you? It will never look like you expect it to look. That's how you know it is God's. So start down that path. One step is all it takes to get started as you look for your Father's treasure.

Your inheritance is waiting!

IS THE REVOLUTION STILL ON?

. . . the kingdom of heaven has been forcefully advancing, and forceful men lay hold of it.[34]
—Jesus

I was at a lunch meeting a few months ago when our guest speaker, a distinguished Briton in his sixties, asked us a question I still can't get out of my head: "Is the revolution still on?"

The question startled me. It woke up something inside of me that had been sleeping. This man looked nothing like a revolutionary to me, but as he spoke I was more and more compelled to think about my own life.

He went on, "Any twenty-year-old can be a revolutionary. In fact, if you aren't, there may be something wrong with you. The real challenge lies in keeping that heart after the idealism of the twenties navigates college, the corporate world, marriage, mortgage payments, diapers, and retirement planning."

Every month his lifelong friend asks him this question as a reminder of what life is ultimately about: "Is the revolution still on?" The question puts everything in perspective.

Webster defines revolution as "a repudiation or upheaval of an established system, characterized by radical change." It comes from the Latin world revolve, which literally means to "roll back" or "turn back." Roll back to what?

How the world is supposed to be.

It's William Wilberforce working fifty years to abolish slavery in the British Empire. It's Mother Teresa giving dignity to the dying in one of the poorest, most forgotten regions of the world for more than forty years. It's watching the Berlin Wall come down, seeing freedom triumph over tyranny after almost thirty years.

These examples in history make us want to stand up and shout, "Yes!" There is something so just, so pure, and so holy that you know you want to be part of something like this for the rest of your life. We are here to change the world: to roll things back to what they are supposed to be.

Look around. Where do you see the values of the world crushing people? Where is justice excluded? Where is compassion absent? A revolutionary can't sit back and just watch that happen. A revolutionary takes a stand against the established system.

Jesus was the greatest revolutionary who ever lived. He introduced a kingdom that changed everything. A kingdom built on justice and compassion—one that resisted greed and tyranny and instead championed love, humility, and forgiveness. He challenged established systems that were corrupted by discrimination. He exposed the shell of spirituality, calling it what it was—an act.

In a way, all those who call themselves followers of Christ are involved in an ongoing insurgency against the world order. Jesus said that "the kingdom of heaven has been forcefully advancing, and forceful men lay hold of it."[35] It is really an invitation—an invitation to a radical way of living.

What in your world needs change? What one thing grieves your spirit? Homelessness. Poverty. Racism. Corporate greed. Slavery. Abandoned children. Children in crisis.

If you are overwhelmed with life as it is, your excuses for ignoring this invitation are probably many, but I want you to consider one revolutionary thought:

this may be your only way back—back to a life that has real meaning.

This revelation could fade. So to keep it alive, do what I did. Ask your good friends to ask you this question a month from now when you forget this chapter (because you will) and see where the question takes you.

Is the revolution still on?

YOU

"Men occasionally stumble over the truth, but most of them pick themselves up and hurry off as if nothing had happened."
—Winston Churchill

So this is the end of the book. Where do you go from here?

Forgive my boldness when I tell you that if it stops with just a feeling, then I almost wish you hadn't picked up this book. As a pastor, I interact daily with people who have the best of intentions, but more often than not, good intentions lead to nothing at all. This book was written to lead you to action, to serve as a catalyst. Take a minute and ask yourself a few questions:

What if no one had responded to the need ten years ago? Irene hadn't knocked? Pastor Bob hadn't prayed? The Stacy Foundation hadn't invested?

What if there was no clear vision? No SafePlace? No place for an eighteen-year-old like Mez to call home? No place for a girl in a crisis pregnancy to turn?

What if no one seized the moment or invested or followed their passion? No Father of the Year for Scott. No Angel for Maurice. No one to keep a promise to Juan. No transformation for Gabrielle.

Thousands of lives would still be broken, lost. Hundreds of sons and daughters would still be orphans. One God would still be waiting for one to be a voice. But that is not the case. Each of these ones made a decision to act. And each decision led to subsequent decisions that changed the world for thousands.

So what about you? What if . . . you close this book and the emotions fade. Your good intentions get distracted. You feel guilty, but never get started. Your sympathy never turns into compassion.

Ultimately you never act—nothing really changes.

If you've learned anything about the one factor, I hope you've learned that it doesn't passively occur in the mind; it has to be passionately lived out in your life.

Otherwise you're just a spectator.

So what is the biggest problem in your community? What is the biggest problem in your world? I want you to write that problem down. Next to it, I want you to write one thing you can do about the problem. Then, I invite you to turn the page. (You're not thinking about reading on before you've grabbed your pen, are you?)

Imagine . . . if you actually did what you wrote down (and the one factor did the rest).

Millions would applaud.

Thousands would be different.

But ONE would cheer louder than the rest.

Because you said yes to your Father.

Now comes the mystery.

—Henry Ward Beecher

Regardless of what your one thing is or even if you're not sure, I would love the chance to provide you with information, ideas, and a person to cheer you on. If you have your own experience with the one factor to share, contact us at: **www.HowOneChangesEverything.com**

All these people, ideas, and moments are intimately connected to the Source of the one factor. If you are curious or have questions about how God works in the lives of people just like you, or if you want to rediscover the Source for yourself, log onto: **www.GodSpeaks.com**

If you would like more information about how one can change your community, log onto **www.4KidsofSFL.org**

EPILOGUE

In the twelve months since the first printing of *The One Factor*, hundreds of people have embraced the challenge and taken that first step. They have done their one thing—and lived to tell about it. The total impact is hard to quantify, because like the one factor, that first step takes on a life of its own. Responses have come from as far east as New Jersey to as far west as California. They've come from way up in Alaska all the way down to Texas. Here are a few of those stories:

Soon after we met at a national conference on orphans, Shirley purchased several cases of *The One Factor*. She numbered each of the books and distributed them freely to those attending foster care presentations, including area pastors and state workers. Her only requirement was after they read it, they had to pass their copy on and e-mail back their thoughts of the book. The reports from this pay it forward-type project are still coming in. (Shirley's plan didn't work exactly as expected as many of the recipients wanted to keep their copy so they ordered additional copies to pass on.) One of the first e-mail responses was from an inspired 7th grade teacher at an inner city school. The teacher was so challenged by *The One Factor* that she contacted us to order copies for each of her co-workers as

a reminder that one person really can make a difference.
www.OliveCrest.org

Stacy is an accomplished competitor and trainer who competed with her horse, Fidelis, at the Olympic level. After working with children at KidsPlace, Stacy was inspired to combine her love of horses with her growing awareness of the emotional needs of foster children. At the ripe age of 21, Stacy began The Fidelis Foundation, an organization that uses equestrian therapy to give wounded children the confidence to move past their abuse. Hundreds of kids have come through their doors in just the first two years—giving them the breakthrough to learn to trust again.
www.Fidelis-Foundation.org

Sharon, a foster mother, used Facebook, an internet social networking site, to promote foster care. Using the "Cause" application on the website, Sharon celebrated her birthday by requesting friends and family contribute to a local foster care agency in lieu of buying her gifts. Her "Facebook-Meets-Foster-Care" idea has gone from one connection to over a thousand connections, as others are following suit.
www.Facebook.com (Join Cause: 4KIDS of South Florida)

Dee read *The One Factor* from cover to cover while on an airplane. It was the title that drew her in. She realized that she could be *One.* Upon returning home, Dee resigned from her position with a non-profit in order to pursue her passion—helping victims of sexual abuse find healing. Trees of Hope is now meeting the needs of the sexually broken in South Florida, taking them from secret shame to redemption.
www.TreesOfHope.org

Dan and his wife had just started their own business. Dee was a single mom with a heart to help foster kids. Their daughters played basketball at the same school and they got to know each other. Dan heard Dee's passion and shared her dream with his business partner. Together their families decided to use their business to support Dee's vision and a few months later, Dee's House was born. They found a home on the same street as their home, and now it is full of toddlers in foster care. Three families united by one vision, in one neighborhood have caught the bug. The whole block may be next.

www.DeesHouse.org

Many of you have asked about some of the people and ministries you met in the pages of *The One Factor.* Here are some updates on them.

TAYLOR'S CLOSET

Lindsay outgrew her 200-square-foot store and is now expanding to a 4,200 square-foot-building, complete with a café and spacious "hang-out" area. Her dad describes it best: "Just think about it. Three years ago, we started out by serving 12 girls in a makeshift "store" aboard a yacht at Christmas time. This year we will minister to more than 950 girls, give away more than 6,300 items of really nice clothing, partner with 25 other ministries, be actively working in 12 cities in seven states and have a footprint in three different countries. And we're just getting started. Recently God put something on our heart that is way bigger than anything we could ever do on our own. But we believe it's from God. So we believe it's achievable. There are 32,000 girls in South Florida who are considered to be "at risk." We want to reach every one of them with the transforming love of the Father. It's gonna happen!"

www.TaylorsCloset.org

THE HEART GALLERY

Since its inception in 2001, the Heart Gallery has grown to over 60 exhibits in 45 states. In some areas the rate of foster care adoptions has more than doubled after the exhibit has been displayed, providing open arms and forever families to children in need.

www.HeartGalleryOfBroward.org

GABRIELLE

This young lady got married (I got to officiate!) She and her husband Nate secured scholarships to Moody Bible Institute in Illinois. She is still planning to devote her life to helping other girls caught in the desperate spiral of foster care.

www.Facebook.com (Search: Gabby Grosso)

To read more ways that people are taking that first step and doing that one thing, log on to our blog at www.HowOneChangesEverything.org.

FOR CONSIDERATION

ONE FACTOR

Why is it so easy to overlook the significance of one?

How can you remind yourself not to overlook the potential of one in your daily routine?

ONE VISION

Think of the biggest problem in your community or your world. How can you begin to tackle such a colossal problem?

What gives people the confidence to believe they can take down a giant problem?

Have you ever been part of a company or organization that had a clear, compelling vision? How did that clarity affect your work there?

Have you ever been a part of a company or organization where the vision wasn't clear or where it constantly changed? What effect did that have on its people?

ONE PERSON

Make a list of the five people who have had the most significant impact on your life.

What qualities do they possess that allowed them to make such an impact in your life?

Would anyone put you on his or her list?

Write down the name of one person whose life would benefit from your investment.

ONE MOMENT

Identify two or three crossroads in your life that changed the direction of your life.

What pushed you in one direction as opposed to another?

Are there any crossroads in your life right now?

Discuss the potential impact that your upcoming decision can have on your life.

How can you effectively "seize the day" to serve people around you in need?

ONE IDEA

What was the best idea you ever had?

What keeps you from pursuing your ideas?

Have you ever watched a simple idea grow into a big idea?

What part did timing play in that process?

Where do great ideas come from?

ONE INVESTMENT

What has been the best investment you have ever made?

What did it feel like to watch your investment grow?

Describe the feeling of making a poor investment.

Have you ever tried to trace the impact of your investments?

How many of your investments will live on after you?

ONE PASSION

What are you most passionate about?

Are there any areas on your list that are about helping other people?

How has your passion for something affected those closest to you?

How does hanging out with people who are passionate about similar things affect you?

ONE SOURCE

Identify a time in your life when you overcame impossible odds and you "chased a thousand."

Do you believe something like that can happen again?

How much of that victory do you attribute to chance, or to God's undercover work?

What is God currently spurring you to take on in your life?

What would you have to lay aside if you were to take on this God-given challenge?

How can you get more connected with God?

I have found that there are three stages in every great work of God;
first it is impossible, then it is difficult, and then it is done.
—Hudson Taylor

ENDNOTES

1)   Deuteronomy 32:30

2)   A child enters foster care because of an anonymous phone call to a
state abuse hotline. If the abuse line operator believes there is proba-
ble cause to investigate, she then notifies the county's local child protection unit. Within 24 hours, a uniformed police officer and an
investigator arrive to look into the allegations. If sufficient evidence of
abuse, neglect, or abandonment exists, the child has a few moments
to gather his or her belongings and stuff them into a duffle or garbage
bag. This scene is usually extremely traumatic and often punctuated
by a raging parent's screams and threats as the crying child is placed
into the investigator's car.

    Before assessment centers like SafePlace existed, children were driven
to a downtown government office building where they sat in a cubicle
with a placement worker. The placement worker would often spend
hours and sometimes days attempting to find a bed at a shelter or with
a foster family. The child would sit in the office with the placement
worker as she called looking for an available foster home. This system
of care exposed children to highly confidential details about their case
and the cases of other children. When no placements were available,
children stayed in hotel rooms with an on-call child support worker. In
some cases, children had to sleep in the local juvenile detention center.
In 2000, Child Welfare advocates in South Florida recognized this
tremendous flaw in the system and developed the concept of an as-
sessment center. At this center, kids could be evaluated physically, emotionally, academically, and socially before they were placed into a
shelter or foster home. In Broward County, this 24 hour "super shelter,"
SafePlace, serves children from newborns to teenagers until they can
find a home with a relative, in an available foster home, or in a shelter.

3)   Within 24 hours of a child's removal from his or her home, a judge
conducts a shelter hearing to determine whether there is sufficient evidence to remove the child from his or her biological parent(s). The
parents appear in court, but are rarely able to leave with their child.
Just under half of the children find placement with a relative or friend
of the family. The other half enters the foster care system for what will
likely be an 18-month stay.

    Several weeks after the first hearing, the parents and lawyer meet
with a representative of the State Attorney's office and a caseworker

to construct a re-unification plan. This plan may require the parents to attend parenting or anger management classes, enter a drug treatment program, get a job, and/or find stable housing. A judge is then presented this plan and officially adjudicates (declares) the child as a dependent of the state. This means the state is now the "parent" of the child and officially charged with his or her care.

Every 90 days the parents' progress is reviewed. Federal law mandates that the child be re-united with the biological parents or be in the process of being adopted within thirteen months. Everyone agrees that long stays in foster care are detrimental to the child, the parents, and the foster parents. Although 13 months is the legal standard, children often languish in foster care for two to three years. If he is lucky, a child will be assigned a guardian ad litem who serves as a court-appointed advocate, working to ensure that the child's best interest remains a priority.

4) Calvary Chapel Fort Lauderdale
5) Psalm 27:5 (NLT)
6) Proverbs 24:3–4
7) John 14:2–3
8) Psalm 68:5–6 (NLT)
9) John 14:18
10) Matthew 10:39
11) Romans 12:15
12) Romans 12:15
13) Psalm 27:10
14) Acts 20:35
15) Deuteronomy 24
16) Mark 4
17) Romans 13:11 (NKJV)
18) 1 Samuel 1, 2
19) 1 Chronicles 11
20) Deuteronomy 32:30
21) Deuteronomy 32:30
22) Isaiah 45:15
23) Leviticus 26:8
24) 2 Peter 1:4
25) John 10:10
26) 1 Corinthians 2:9
27) Psalm 68:6
28) Matthew 6:10
29) John 17:20–21
30) Psalm 133
31) Ezekiel 16
32) Matthew 25:40
33) Ephesians 1:3–5
34) Matthew 11:12
35) Matthew 11:12